The Poets of the Powers

The Poets of the Powers

Magic, Freedom, and Renewal

Kamil V. Zvelebil

Integral Publishing
1993

First published by Rider & Co., London, 1973

Printed in the United States of America.

Published by Integral Publishing
P.O. Box 1030
Lower Lake, California 95457

Cover design by Brenda Plowman and Dawson Church
Atrium Publishing Group, Lower Lake, California

Zvelebil, Kamil.
The poets of the powers : magic, freedom, and renewal / Kamil V. Zvelebil
p. cm.
Originally published: London : Rider, 1973
ISBN 0-941255-32-8 : $12.95
1. Tamil Siddhas. 2. Tamil poetry--History and criticism.
I. Title.
BL2032.T3Z9 1993
294.5'5--dc20
92-33629
CIP

Printing (last digit) 9 8 7 6 5 4 3 2 1

A Tamil Siddha

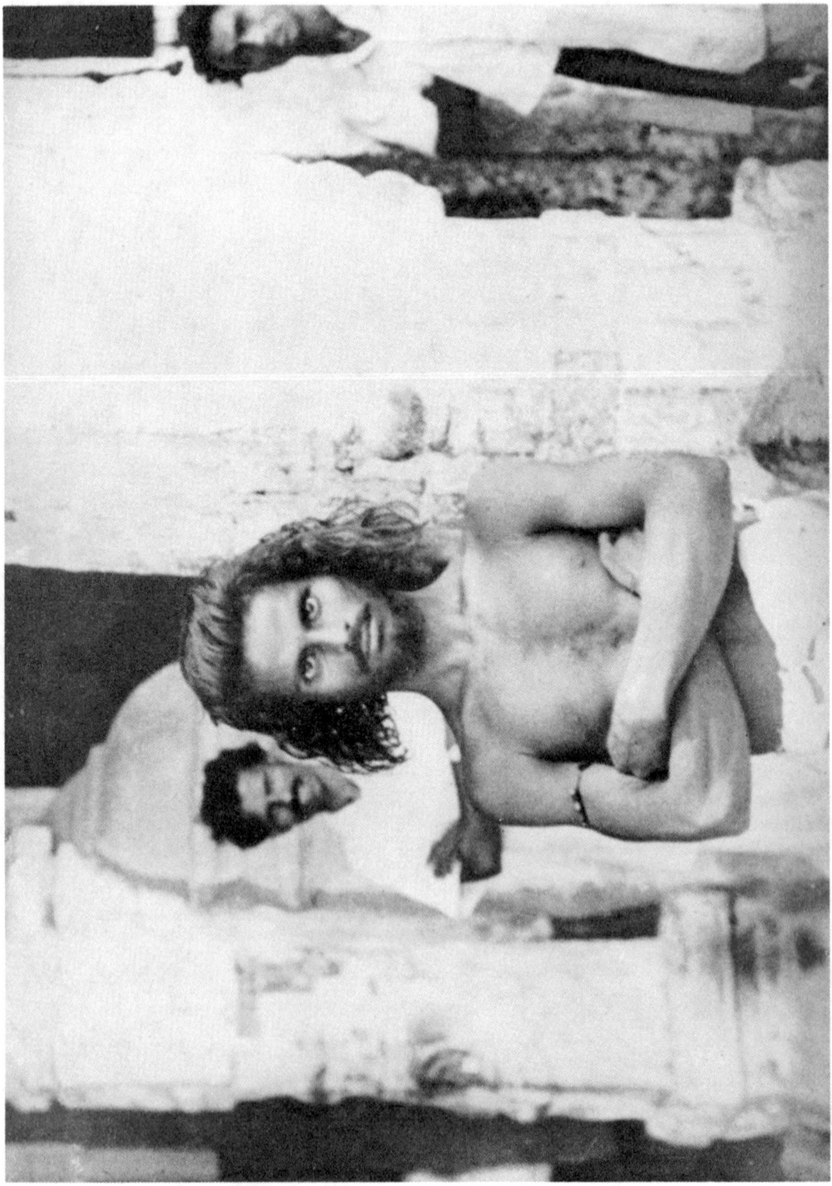

M. V. Venugopala Pillai

Contents

Contents

Foreword

'There is no more absorbing story than that of the discovery and interpretation of India by Western consciousness' (Mircea Eliade).

Many and variegated are the contributions of the Tamils of South India[1] to the treasures of human civilization. The early classical love and war poetry, the architecture of the Pallavas, the deservedly famous South Indian bronzes of the Chola period, the intricate school of vocal and instrumental music known as the Carnatic system, the well-known Bharata Natyam dance, the philosophy of *Saiva Siddhānta*, the magnificent temples of the South—for more than two thousand years have the Tamils been contributing to Indian culture and taking part in shaping and moulding the great Indian synthesis.

One of the most perplexing and fascinating pages in the history of their culture is found in the compositions ascribed to the Siddhas (Tamil *cittar*). Their writings, as well as their thoughts and ideas in the fields of religion, philosophy, medicine, alchemy and Yoga, belong to the most thrilling, even sensational but, at the same time, the darkest and almost unknown chapters in the history of Indian thought. It is a very provocative puzzle: the flashes of exceptional knowledge and deep wisdom, and the social and philosophical context of Siddha writings are so stimulating and exciting that one feels compelled to investigate the matter and try to unravel its mysteries. Besides, some *cittar* poems are truly great poetry.

Almost all of the writings of the Tamil Siddhas claim that

their authors have achieved certain psychokinetic powers and other capabilities which belong to the sphere of parapsychologic phenomena; almost all of them manifest a protest, expressed often in very strong terms, against the formalities of life and religion; denial of religious practices and beliefs of the ruling classes; social radicalism and opposition against the generally accepted pan-Indian social and religious doctrines; almost all of them may be characterized as puritanical and monotheistic; but, at the same time, many of them use a language which is very imaginative, ambiguous, obscure, puzzling, often vulgar and even obscene.

The present volume is, as far as I know, the first monograph dedicated to the Tamil Siddhas—apart from a short book written by an Indian scholar about fifteen years ago which does not contain any samples of their writings and deals with their thought in rather superficial manner.[2] Opinions about the writings of the Tamil Siddhas differ greatly, even radically. An early writer on the history of Tamil literature, Purnalingam Pillai, says at the beginning of this century: 'They are most popular works in Tamil and there is no pure Tamilian, educated or uneducated, who has not committed to memory at least a few stanzas from one or another of them . . . Their aim was to get at the eternal light . . . They were the haters of the Aryan social fabric, religious rites, and the Vedic authority and were addicted to opium eating . . . they formed the noblest order who viewed the Vedanta and Siddhanta alike.'

M. Srinivassa Aiyangar writes in 1914 'They were yogis as well as medical men . . . Most of them were plagiarists and impostors, while some assumed the names of the great men of antiquity like Agastyar, Kapilar, and Tiruvalluvar. Being eaters of opium and dwellers in the land of dreams, their conceit knew no bounds . . . Their religion was theism; sometimes the stress they laid on the *siddhis* or powers a man can acquire over nature gave it a secularist colour which occasionally comes very near atheism and may be mistaken for it.'

C. and H. Jesudasan, in *A History of Tamil Literature* (1961), call the Siddhas a 'remarkable group of free thinkers' and go on to say: 'The *cittars* were, on the whole, a fascinating body of revolutionaries who refused to allow themselves to be carried away by the spirit of the religion of the times . . . It is evident that they commanded great respect among the people by the force of their personalities and their ideas.'

Such difference of opinion should by itself arouse our curiosity and prompt us to investigate the matter closely. Even more provocative are the Siddha stanzas.

> 'We can lift the Eight Big Mountains throwing them about;
> all the Seven Oceans drink and spit them out;
> enter burning fire, and waters, and a tiger fight',

boasts 'The Siddha with the Dancing Snake' (*Pāmpāṭṭi Cittar*) in one of his songs (written sometime between the 12th–14th Century A.D.). And he goes on, employing the obscene diction characteristic of some of these strange poets: 'We can change men into women and pricks into cunts!' This is, indeed, hardly any poetry; nor the following lines either:

> 'We can transform all the Three Worlds into shining gold,
> we can even ruin and ravage all this immense world,
> we can flatten, overpower, subjugate the King!
> We can make new splendid creatures like those made by God,
> we can live on equal footing with the Lord of Lords!'

Is this a mad bragging of a deranged mind, or did the Siddha really believe, on some experimental grounds, that he and his mystical brothers were capable of such enormous and preponderant deeds? Or is it all only symbolic language, intended to cover some other, hidden meaning?

But there is, as stressed above, also true poetry in the writings of the Siddhas:

'When the Carpenter of Time
will fell,
like trees which are broken and bruised,
the bodies of men and women
who clasp each other in close embrace,
they will cry out
and weep
like a stricken drum.
Will they cross the cremation ground
and reach the land
beyond?'

Paṭṭiṉattār, who is the author of these lines, has also sung

'The eightfold Yoga
The six regions of the body
The five states
They all have left and gone
Totally erased
And in the open
Void
I am left
Amazed.
There is but a red rounded Moon
A fountain of white milk
For delight
The unobtainable Bliss
Has engulfed me
A precipice
Of light.'

The present author is an expert in South Indian philology and in Tamil linguistics and literature, and an Indologist. He had a chance to become personally acquainted with the living Siddha tradition in the South of India in 1968 and this small monograph is the result of his study of the texts, and his personal experience. It does not claim any new substantial contribution to the fields of Indian religion and philosophy which are, for the author, only of oblique interest.[3]

Concluding the foreword one can do no better than quote from what M. Eliade wrote in 1954 about Yoga: 'It is essential that we know and understand a thought that has held a place of the first importance in the history of universal spirituality. And it is essential that we know it *now*. For, on the one hand, it is from *now* on that, any cultural provincialism having been outstripped by the very course of history, we are forced—Westerners and non-Westerners alike—to think in terms of universal history and to forge universal spiritual values. And, on the other hand, it is *now* that the problem of man's situation in the world dominates the philosophical consciousness of Europe.'

Note on Transliteration and Pronunciation

The transcription used for Tamil words in this book is a strict transliteration, a system adopted by the Madras University *Tamil Lexicon*. The following Roman letters are used for the Tamil characters:

Vowels

Short	Long
a	ā
i	ī
u	ū
e	ē
o	ō

ai au

Consonants

	Lips	*Teeth*	*Ridge behind upper teeth*		*Hard palate*		*Soft palate*
Stops	p	t			ṭ	c	k
Nasals	m	n	ṉ		ṇ	ñ	ṅ
Liquids			r	l	ḷ		
			ṟ		ḻ		
Semivowels	v					y	

Tamil long vowels are simple long vowels, unlike their English diphthongized counterparts. Final –ai is pronounced approximately like –ey.

Tamil has two series of consonants foreign to English speakers: the dentals t, n and the retroflexes ṭ, ṇ, ḷ, ḻ. The dentals are pronounced with the tongue at the teeth, the retroflexes by curling the tongue back towards the roof of the mouth (cf. the American pronunciation of gi*r*l, si*r*).

In the middle of Tamil words, long consonants occur. In transliteration, they are indicated by double letters (e.g. *cittar*). English has long consonants between words, cf. ho*t t*ea.

The Tamil r is flapped or trilled like Spanish or Italian r. The ḻ is somewhat like the American variety of r; r and ṟ are not distinguished by most modern speakers, but long ṟṟ is pronounced like tr in English *tr*ap; ṉṟ is pronounced ndr as in lau*ndr*y.

p, t, ṭ, c, k are pronounced initially as voiceless stops (c being pronounced sometimes as tch, sometimes as sh); between vowels, p, t, ṭ are voiced into b, d and ḍ, and pronounced as lax voiced stops; k and c are pronounced as gh or h and s or sh respectively. After nasals, all stops are voiced into b, d, ḍ, j, g.

Instances: Murukaṉ is pronounced as muruhan, *pāṭal* is pronounced as paadal, *ciṅkaḷavar* as shingalavar, Ceyyōṉ as sheyyoon, *Kantapurāṇam* as kandaburaanam and so on.

I The Personal Account

My first acquaintance with the Tamil Siddhas dates back to 1958. It was a very odd encounter, for it took place in the laundry of Spencer and Co, that ageless establishment on Mount Road in Madras. I was known to the washermen there as a Tamil-speaking *veḷḷaikkārar* ('white man') interested, for reasons of his own, in Tamil culture and literature. One day, one of the laundry-men showed me, with an almost conspiratorial look and with a shy smile on his dark face, a dirty, torn, cheap print of some poems which he declared to be not only absolutely marvellous poetry but, at the same time, the only true teaching about life and death, a guide to liberation, and an instruction on how to achieve true freedom from the human bondage. At that time, I was not interested. The owner of the brochure did not strike me as a particularly happy and free man, and I had a lot to do with my field-work in Tamil dialects. The term he mentioned, *cittar kavitai* 'poetry of the Siddhas', did not convey any meaning to me. I was blind and deaf.

In the same year, however, I met for the first time my Tamil guru, Mahavidvan M. V. Venugopala Pillai. He was giving a series of lectures on Kampaṉ's monumental Tamil epic, 'The Descent of Rāma', and one of my closest Tamil friends, Mr. R. Kannan of Madras, took me along to listen to the great teacher.[4] Venugopala Pillai struck me as a man of absolute integrity and honesty, great and critical learning, and very kind heart. I was not mistaken. I still regard myself, as far as classical

Tamil and Tamil philology and prosody are concerned, as his humble student.

Venugopala Pillai published, among many other texts, an anthology entitled *Cittar ñāṉakkōvai* 'The Garland of Knowledge of the Siddhas'. It was through this book that I became seriously interested in the Tamil Siddha writings.

Thanks to my guru, I also began to understand a few very important fundamental points about the Indian attitude towards knowledge and learning, particularly about 'knowledge of truth' (if there is such a thing). In India, it seems, 'truth' is not precious *an sich*, in itself; it becomes valuable because it helps man to liberate himself. Another aspect of the Indian attitude towards learning is its initiatory stucture: one does not learn by oneself; the guidance of a master, of a guru, is necessary. The pupil, traditionally, learns his texts orally, by heart, from the teacher, who at the same time comments upon them.[5]

A few years after my first trip to India I studied in the library of the British Museum,[6] and there I unearthed quite a number of Tamil Siddha texts, both published (mostly as cheap 'folk' editions, beginning roughly with the last one or two decades of the 19th Century), and unpublished (on palm-leaves). That, however, is a matter to be discussed in a different and more technical publication.

Finally, in 1967–68, I met a 'live' Siddha to whom I owe much of what I know about the Tamil school of the *cittar*, and who initiated me into the 'intentional language' of the texts. I had several occasions to witness his 'powers' (*siddhi*), some of which were indeed of very high achievement. My Siddha informant insisted that he belonged to the line of *Yākkopu* (Yākūb, Jacob), one of the two originators of the Tamil system of *cittavaittiyam*, Siddha medicine. Being a devotee of Murukaṉ,[7] he spends his life between Paḻaṉi (a place connected intimately with Siddha tradition) and Madras, where he has a medical practice as a Siddha physician. That is as far as I can go in identifying him.

2 *The Texts and the Authors*

One of the central problems—if not *the* central problem—humanity has always had to face, is the problem of human historicity, temporality and limitability; the fact that man is 'conditioned' by time and space, that he is mortal, that he is limited. In short, the quest for immortality and freedom is the human quest *par excellence*.

There have been many different solutions to this problem, as one would expect. One can accept stoically the inevitable, in harmony with the rhythm of life and death, take things as they come, 'peacefully and with a calm mind', and live so that 'the earlier acts of our lives will be proved on the touchstone of our last breath'; the attitude of the 'philosopher'.[8]

Another, and the most usual solution in Western civilization and in our times, is the empirico-historical attitude, the attitude of the scientist, leading mankind to the conquest of nature, sickness, and space. The removal of social evils through revolution or evolution—man ever expanding, ever perfecting his technology, his power, man looking back into his own history and prehistory, and forward, into the future, man planning his future; in short, accepting his historicity and temporality as an individual, but attempting to conquer it as mankind. Man, as individual, according to this view, is limited and mortal; but mankind, for all practical purposes, is immortal and can be made free.[9]

There have been other answers, magic for instance, and art. Even fairy-tales are an attempt to answer this basic problem, through 'recovery, escape, and consolation': recovery, 're-gaining of a clear view'; the escape from death in fantasy; the 'eucatastrophic' consolation of the joy of the happy ending.[10]

India has also offered its specific answer, its method how to abolish time and history, how to conquer freedom and immortality: to live outside of time, to become free, liberated in life, and hence 'deconditioned' and immortal through the conquest of the superconscious by specific techniques, by a practice which replaces our false experience by 'true' enstatic experience leading to deliverance.

The Tamil *cittar* (Siddha) school of thought is one of the most important and interesting off-shoots of the pan-Indian tantric Yoga movement. It is more than worth-while and interesting to make oneself acquainted with it.

However, at the very outset one is faced with a very basic difficulty; the general inaccessibility of the sources, of the *texts*.

The Tamil Siddha texts have, so far, not been published at all *in toto*, and in a critical or even a near-to-critical manner. It is first of all necessary to realize that obviously a vast amount of widely differing literature covering many centuries has been called 'the writings of the *cittar*'. If we compare lists of Tamil Siddha authors there is a basic core of names which keep recurring (like for example Akattiyar, Civavākkiyar or Pāmpāṭṭic Cittar), but there are also names which occur only once; no two lists are exactly alike. One may say, though, that most sources agree that there were 18 Tamil Siddhas possessing the 'eight great powers' (*siddhi*).[11] The basic 'core' of this group of thinkers and poets will be discussed in some length later. On the other hand it is equally clear that at least three rather different groups of authors are lumped together under the term *cittar* (Siddhas), since they have a few basic properties in common; but we have to distinguish among them and set them apart.

Let me stress at the very beginning that this distinction is not based on chronology—for two reasons: one being simply our inability (at the present state of research) to set up more than a very approximate relative chronology of the main *cittar* authors. The other reason is deeper and more interesting.

One often hears that India, in contrast to 'the West' (a rather vague term, but quite useful sometimes), disregards historical approach, and ignores history in general. The fact is that the importance of chronology must indeed not be exaggerated; for, in India, any treatise contains conceptions which antedate its composition (and are often quite astonishingly old). It is extremely difficult to establish the dates of different texts, and even more difficult to set up the chronology of religious or philosophical ideologies. One of the reasons is that Indian authors rarely present a personal system. They are usually content to formulate traditional doctrines in the idiom of their day. Hence a rebuke of plagiarism is absolutely off the mark; thus for example the Tamil Siddhas 'assumed the names of the great men of antiquity' not because they were 'impostors' but precisely because they were not interested in formulating personal systems; on the contrary, they wanted to establish the continuity with the 'prehistoric' and 'a-historic', that is perpetual, eternal 'revelation'. For, according to Indian tradition, the historical context of a 'revelation' has only minor value (if it is given any value at all); historical moments only formulate, in the appropriate language of the age, a timeless message.

This, of course, complicates matters immensely, for us, who, with our prevailing empirico-historical outlook, are always interested in the evolution and historical sequence of doctrines.

Anyhow, it is obvious that, as mentioned above, at least three groups of thinkers are denoted as Siddhas in Tamil culture:

(1) A group of alchemists and physicians, who have com-

posed in Tamil a vast number of alchemic and medical treatises, both in verse and prose, and who belonged to what is termed *cittavaittiyam* or 'Siddha medicine' and *cittaracavātam* or 'Siddha alchemy'; e.g. Kōrakkar and his 100 stanzas of *Kōrakkar vaippu*.

(2) A group of thinkers and poets who have composed a large but better manageable number of stanzas in Tamil, more or less based on tantric Yoga in outlook and religious philosophy and practice, between roughly the 10th–15th Centuries A.D., e.g. Tirumūlar and his *Tirumantiram* or Civavākkiyar and his *Pāṭal*.

(3) A few 'Siddha-like' poets who have been 'appended' to the Siddha school by posterior generations, or who called themselves *cittar* without properly belonging to the esoteric group itself: e.g. Paṭṭiṉattār (15th Century?) or Tāyumāṉavar (17th Century).

Now, the texts ascribed to the first group of the Tamil Siddha alchemists, magicians, yogins and physicians, are scattered in a large number of cheap prints, which have been appearing for approximately the last 80–90 years; a vast number of such texts exists still unprinted, on palm-leaves, all over the South of India, as well as in some libraries in the West, like the library of the British Museum or Copenhagen's Royal Library, the Bibliothéque nationale in Paris, the Vatican library and so on. The so-called Mackenzie Collection (BM 620.g.34) contains for example a long list of items connected directly or indirectly with the Siddhas (e.g. Agastya's 'autobiography' plus a list of 38 works ascribed to him, or the 'Forty-Eight Verses on the Cure of Gonorrhea', etc.).

Some of the second group of works, comprising those of the Tamil Siddha *poets*, 'the poets of powers', as we have chosen to call them, have been anthologized and published in printed editions, the earliest of such editions being probably Ramalinga Mudaliyar's *Periya ñāṉakkōvai*, 'The Great Garland of Knowledge' of 1899, in 2 volumes. Nowadays—apart from cheap prints of individual Siddha poets, such as I was shown by the washerman at Spencer's—there exist at least two anthologies of their poetry available, one published in 1947 and reprinted in 1956,[12] another published in 1959, reprinted in 1963 and 1968.[13] This group of poets is our chief concern in this monograph, plus one poet of the third group, probably the greatest *poet* of all, Paṭṭiṉattār.

However, as stressed above, the problems of chronology, critical arrangement and classification of the authors and their works, have not yet in fact been even touched let alone discussed seriously, and this is certainly not the place to discuss them. The obvious first pre-requisite for any further serious scholarly work on the Tamil Siddhas is to unearth all unpublished (manuscript) texts and to collect all published texts together, and prepare an annotated catalogue of such works. As the next step, a critical edition of, at least, the basic *cittar* works may be contemplated. Until this step is taken and finished, we have to rest content with the editions which we have and contemplate the texts which are accessible to us, however fragmentary and imperfect the picture may be.

The fact that the compositions of the Tamil Siddhas are so little known to literary history, to the historiography of science in India, and to Indology in general, is also due to the neglect and disregard of this fascinating body of texts. But why this neglect, why this disregard? Has it been only fortuitous, only incidental, or are there some valid reasons for it which can be dealt with?

There are at least two very good reasons for the fact that, thus far, scholarship has been relatively ignorant of the Tamil Siddha tradition: first, the deep-rooted prejudice *against* the Siddhas among orthodox Hindus in Tamilnadu itself; and second, the fact that the Siddha doctrines have been guarded as an esoteric teaching.

Hindu orthodoxy in the South (generally 'more' orthodox than in the North of India) has always tended to ignore the *cittar* doctrines, even to suppress them. The works of the Siddhas were uncared for, neglected, falsified and even destroyed. 'I was told some years ago,' writes W. Taylor in his *A Catalogue Raisoneé of Oriental Manuscripts*, 3 vols., Madras, 1857–62, 'that the ascetics (Paṇḍārams) of the Śaiva class seek after copies of this poem (i.e. Civavākkiyar's *Pāṭal*) with avidity and uniformly destroy every copy they find. It is in consequence rather scarce and chiefly preserved by native Christians'.[14] And A. V. Subramania Aiyar, in the above quoted monograph, says: 'The prejudice of the orthodox Saivites against the Tamil Siddhars was deep-rooted. They either ignored them or looked down upon them though the Siddhars also accepted Lord Siva as their Supreme God. . . . This prejudice . . . resulted in the texts of the works of the Siddhars, excepting that of Tirumular, being uncared for and neglected' (p. vii).

It is only very recently that the Siddha doctrine is, so to say, being 'rehabilitated', but certainly not among the orthodox Hindu Śaiva and Vaiṣṇava circles; works of the *cittar* are nowadays being accepted by a section of the intellectuals as the expression of 'pure' Tamil indigenous thought, as *the* Tamil medicine, *the* Tamil philosophy and so on. However, among the not so very orthodox masses in the South of India, the Siddha undercurrent has always been very strong, as a part of the entire yogico-alchemical folklore, of the mythology of the yogin-magician, making use of an elixir of immortality, floating in the air, scoffing at the 'establishment', inflating another's body with his breath, making himself invisible, having the power to restore the capacity for juvenile activities including unlimited cohabitation and so on.

One of the consequences of the fact that the Siddha doctrines have always been considered an esoteric teaching which may be revealed only in the initiatory manner, by oral instruction, through a guru, is the type of *enigmatic language* in which some parts of these 'closed' texts are composed. What Giuseppe Tucci has to say[15] about the *dohā* verses of tantric literature is true about the majority of Tamil Siddha poems: they are 'initiatic lyrics in which the mystic, with a terminology understandable only by his spiritual brethren, sings of his ecstasies and hints, in devious terms, at his laborious and blissful conquests'. Tamil Siddha texts, too, are often composed in dark, ambiguous language, or rather in a language in which words are on purpose semantically polyvalent. The term 'twilight language' was proposed for such diction (Haraprasād Śāstrī, 1916). Another term, suggested by Vidhushekar Shastri, is 'intentional language'.[16] The texts seek to conceal the doctrine from the uninitiate; they can be read with a number of keys: liturgical, yogic, tantric, but also as plain and simple songs, almost as folk-songs (some of them). We have to make a distinction, at least as far as the Tamil Siddha poems go, between 'diction' and 'language'. The diction is often enigmatic (Burnouf), mysterious (Kern), hidden (M. Müller), full of analogies, metaphors, symbols and double meanings; but the language the texts employ, in its syntax and lexicon, is more often than not almost vulgar; at any rate, it is a simple, colloquial idiom, close to the speech of the masses. Thus such verses can address people at many levels of training and spiritual awareness; one and the same line sounds, to a casual listener, like a simple folk-song of a snake-charmer; to a tantric adept, it may convey an instruction how to act to attain liberation. The verses seem to be intended for both. This means that we are dealing with a literature which *operates on more than one level.*

Also, since doctrinal teachings and discursive knowledge are explicitly refuted by the Siddhas, the texts themselves do not usually state anything explicitly or discursively, but rather in images, metaphors, allusions, ambiguously and vaguely, and most unconventionally. Also sexual symbolism is frequently employed.

Finally, as Eliade says (*op. cit.* 250): the 'destruction of [normal, regular] language contributes, in its way, too, toward "breaking" the profane universe and replacing it by a universe of convertible and integrable planes'.

At this point I shall give just a few illustrations from the Tamil Siddha texts to show how this kind of 'intentional language' works in them, and some instances of the sexual symbolism and the obscene diction.

Akappēy Cittar, 'the Siddha [who sings about] the Demon of the Soul', has a quatrain (47) which says:

> 'The delicious nectar of the Moon—listen, O Demon of the Soul—
> will flow [into] the poison of the Sun,
> the Whiteness of the Moon—listen, O Demon of the Soul—
> will turn into the Vermilion of the Sun.—'

For the 'uninitiated', casual listener, this stanza conveys almost no sense. There is no commentary on this text. But according to my Siddha informant, and in agreement with the tantric traditions preserved in other texts,[17] this 'surface' meaning is of course not the 'true' meaning of the stanza. The tantric adept knows that the Moon stands for *semen virile* (and also for the 'left channel', 'left nostril', 'perfect wisdom' etc.; the Moon '*is born*' of the sperm, which is of the essence of Śiva); while the Sun symbolizes the menstrual fluid, the *rajas*, the blood of women (also 'right channel', 'right nostril', etc.; the Sun '*is born*' of the ovum; blood is of the essence of Śakti and the Sun). Hence the stanza deals actually with the unification of semen and blood, of Śiva and Śakti, of left and right 'conduits', of Sun and Moon, which means the 'conjunction of opposites', that is the abolishment of all experience of duality, that is the transcending of the phenomenal world—in other words, the destruction of the cosmos, the return to the original Unity. At the same time, the stanza is an instruction how to act: the tantric Yoga technique intended here is the sexual union conceived as a ritual.

In the Tamil texts, the numeral *añcu* 'five' is one of those polysemantic items which may signify a great number of things: the five senses, or the five elements, the five 'states' (*avattai*), the five qualities of Śiva, the five *kośas* or 'bodies' of Yoga (the gross physical body, the subtle body, the desire-mind body, the body of wisdom, and the body of bliss), but also the mystical utterance (*mantra*) of five 'letters' (*ci-vā-ya-na-ma*). This use of the numeral 'five' in many esoteric meanings is very typical of Tirumūlar's *Tirumantiram* (see below).

The mystical *mantra* (utterance) of five syllables is the subject of the following enigmatic stanza by the foremost Tamil Siddha Civavākkiyar.[18]

> 'Like so many forms he stands, by reason of the sound *a*,
> having dressed himself in shapes, by reason of the sound *u*,
> the illusory world, by reason of the sound *ma*;
> the *civāyam* became realized, by reason of the sound *ci*.'

This may indeed seem 'closed by the lock of ignorance'. However: the sound *a* (*akāram*) is the symbol of beginning, and of the Primeval Lord who is eternal and omnipresent; the sound *u* stands for *uru*, *uruvu* (Sanskrit *rūpa*) which means 'shape, form', i.e. material shapes of the phenomenal world; the sound *ma* symbolizes *mayakkam* 'bewilderment, confusion, illusion', also *māyā* 'cosmic illusion, illusion of creation'; and *ci-* is of course the first syllable of *civāyam*, i.e. *na-ma-ci-vā-yam*, the sacred 'five letters', the mystic formula of Śaivism and Siddhism. In other words, the quatrain contains an entire theology: God is the eternal and omnipresent Being, the true essence of all *Ens*, clad in material forms, existing as phenomenal world because of illusion and ignorance, which is dispelled by the mystic teaching and practice of *namacivāyam*, and *civayām* is realized. Schematically:

a= Supreme Lord, Primeval Being.
u= in endless material forms.
m(*a*)= existing as phenomenal world because of *māyā*.
ci= removed by the doctrine and practice of *civayām*.

Reading the first 'letters' of the quatrain vertically, we get again the greatest and most potent *mantra*: *a*+ *u*+ *m*+ *ci*= *aum*, i.e. *oṃ ci*(*vāyanama*).

I mentioned above the fact that, frequently, sexual imagery and vulgarity, even obscenity, are quite characteristic features of the ambiguous, 'intentional' language of Siddha texts. The first point can be illustrated by the verses of Saraha, the great Buddhist tantric teacher of about 750 A.D. (writing in a form of Proto-Bengali), who says that describing the Highest Experience would be so futile 'like describing sexual pleasure (*surata*) to a virgin'.

The second feature of 'vulgarity' and/or 'obscenity' of the Siddha language may be illustrated by the following stanza of Pāmpāṭṭic Cittar ('The Siddha with the Dancing Snake'):[19]

> 'They will compare
> the bare and desiccated skin
> of those round breasts to the Mēru Mount.
> And you, o dancing snake,
> are sure that they will perish—
> those who fell
> into the well of a stinking cunt!'

The insufficiency of all modes of expression had to be gradually accepted in Indian mystic literature—as everywhere else (Mystics, it had been said, have neither birthday nor native land). From the imagery of symbolism (including sexual symbolism, and vulgar or even obscene imagery) to the notion of *light* and *bliss* (e.g. *parañcōti* 'Supreme Light', or *veṭṭa veḷi* 'broad daylight' in the Tamil texts) and the notions of *silence*[20], and *void*;[21] finally, nothing remains to express the idea of divinity but *pure negation*.[22] [23]

3 *Tamil Siddhas in India*

'We must bear in mind that the yogins and *saddhus* contributed to the spiritual unification of India, both by their journeys throughout the country and by their monasteries and sacred places. Although they were divided into countless sects, their ascetic techniques and mystical itineraries differed very little.' (M. Eliade, *op. cit.* 424.)

(1) One of the reasons why the study of the Tamil Siddha thought has so far been only superficial, fragmentary and unsuccessful derives probably from the fact that it has not been approached from the right angle and in the right perspective. If mentioned and commented upon at all, this was done in isolation, and not in the context of similar or almost identical movements elsewhere in India. The Siddhas of Tamilnadu are certainly not an isolated and unique body of freethinkers, but an integral part of a pan-Indian tradition.

This is naturally not the place to trace the entire development of the pan-Indian Siddha movement down to its protohistory and prehistory, to its roots and beginnings. It is indeed highly improbable whether anyone would be able to perform such a feat—at the present state of our knowledge of the matter.

The truth seems to be, however, that the Siddha streams which are inseparable from a larger context of tantric Yoga, are contained, at least *in nuce*, in the very earliest manifestations of Yoga on the Indian soil. Ascetic methods and techniques of ecstasy and enstasy may be found among many peoples; but, as Eliade rightly stresses, Yoga is to be found only in India and in cultures influenced by Indian spirituality. On the Indian soil the ancient and universally disseminated magical tradition reached a full blossoming which was probably unparalleled elsewhere in the world. Now the Siddha stream or streams have their source in a particular branch of Yoga, in *tantric* Toga.

Tantrism undoubtedly contains very old elements, some of which belong to the religious protohistory and prehistory of India; but their introduction or rather intrusion into Buddhism and Hinduism in a more massive and systematic manner began relatively late—not before the first centuries of our era, probably only after the 5th-6th Century A.D. Ancient, 'classical' Yoga, which is not a matter of our concern in this book, was *assimilated into* tantrism, which appeared as a distinct stream as early as the 4th Century A.D., and from about the 5th Century onward spread all over the country, especially in the North-East, and the South.

However, as already stressed, the basic elements of Siddha Yoga can be traced to very early times. Thus already in the rather early *Śvetāśvataropaniṣad* II, 8–13, we may recognize some fundamental elements of Siddhism: 'No sickness, no old age, no death has he/who has obtained a body made out of the fire of Yoga. Lightness, healthiness, steadiness,/clearness of countenance and pleasantness of voice,/sweetness of odour and scanty excretions—/these, they say, are the first stage in the progress of Yoga' (Hume's translation).

In the *Yogatattvopaniṣad* it is for the first time that numerous and precise details are given concerning the extraordinary powers called *siddhi*, and gained by practice and meditation. Thus for example the power of rising into the air is mentioned in this Upaniṣad, or that of controlling and dominating any being; the yogin becomes strong and beautiful, and women desire him; but he must remain chaste, since 'on account of the retention of semen an agreeable smell will be generated in body of the yogin'. A long list of occult powers mentioned in the text shows that this Upaniṣad was composed in a magical milieu; it mentions for instance clairvoyance, travelling across vast distances in short time, making oneself invisible, and the power of transmuting iron into gold by smearing it with the yogin's urine and excreta.

Here, then, is probably one of the roots of the magical physiology, the basis of the mystico-ascetic tradition which takes us ultimately to our Tamil *cittar*. According to the *Yogatattvopaniṣad*, the *siddhis*—the magic powers—are also generated by *mudrās*—gestures—which have therapeutic effect (like disappearance of grey hair); thus for example the power of flying through air, knowledge of the future and even immortality. All these motifs—the pursuance of unlimited longevity, the preoccupation with alchemy, the acquirement of *siddhis*—are indeed diagnostic for our Tamil Siddhas. What is so thrilling about the *Tamil* Siddhas is the fact that this esoteric mystico-ascetic tradition which—as far as our knowledge goes—is attested in Indian texts from the times of the *later* Upaniṣads (composed about the same time as the didactic portions of the *Mahābhārata*, that is, in the first two centuries A.D.) is still very much alive in Tamil India, and considered until this day an esoteric, somewhat dangerous, yet singularly attractive part of the Tamil spiritual heritage.

Who are the Siddhas? Why do we use the term at all? According to Eliade (*op. cit.* 302), the Siddhas are those 'who understood liberation as the conquest of immortality'. Tirumūlar, the greatest exponent of Yoga in Tamil culture, defines the Siddhas as those 'who have experienced divine light (*oḷi*) and divine power (*catti*, Sanskrit *śakti*) from within and through Yogic *samādhi*'.[24]

Thus all yogins who attained 'perfection' can be called Siddhas; but the term Siddhas (Tamil *cittar*) is indeed derived from the term *siddhi*[25] or 'miraculous, magical power', and hence the perfection in question is primarily *magical perfection*.

The *Haṭhayogapradīpikā* (I, 5–9) contains a list of 'great Siddhas'. Some names tend to appear with greater frequency in various sources. In North India, aside from Matsyendranāth and Gorakhnāth, the most important Siddhas are Nāgārjuna and the alchemists. As in the South, there are a few names which tend to reappear again and again: Agastya, Tirumūlar, Civavākkiyar. The number 84 (Siddhas) current in the North is as 'unhistorical' as the number 18 in the South; both are mystical numbers well attested in Indian tradition.

Though the Siddha mythology and folklore is comparatively 'recent' from a strictly chronological point of view, the content they represent is in fact extremely archaic. 'The emergence of spirituality long unknown, and hence unrecorded, by the 'official' cultural circles—that is, by circles more or less dependent upon a learned tradition' (Eliade *op. cit.* 302)—that is the force which is behind the Siddha legends and mythology. 'The popular legends and vernacular literatures created around Gorakhnāth, the Nāthas, and the Siddhas give expression to the real spiritual longings of the superficially Hinduized masses' (*ib.*).

The assimilation of the yogin to the magician was almost inevitable. Looking back at what Pāmpāṭṭic Cittar sings about the unlimited capabilities of the Siddhas (quoted in the *Foreword*), we hear a close echo of Gorakhnāth's lines: 'The might of our religion is such that I control Hari-Hara and the greatest and most ancient of the gods; I stop the course of the planets in the heavens; I submerge the earth in water, with its mountains and cities, and I again drink up the waters in a moment. . . . He who resembles the gods, whose crest is the lunar orb, and who with delight embraces women as beautiful as Pārvatī, feels supreme bliss.'[26] All of the Siddhas in the North of India have legends ascribing to them incredible magic powers: Gorakhnāth fed 25,000 yogins and disciples on a single grain of rice; Hāḍī Siddha recites a mantra on a broom; instantly countless brooms fall from the sky and sweep the market-place. As he sits in the royal park meditating, coconuts fall before him; he drinks the milk and eats the pulp, and lo, the nuts return to their places in the trees; he makes the sun and the moon his earrings, and so on.[27] Many such miracles, as Eliade says, belong to the universal magical tradition, but the most important are probably those which concern the motif of immortality.

And here we finally approach the basic diagnostic feature of Siddhism, of the tantric Siddha Yoga (in contrast to 'classical' Yoga): liberation (Tamil *mutti*, Sanskrit *mukti*) can be gained *only* by setting out from the body; hence it is necessary that the body remains healthy and strong (this is still the position of classical Haṭha Yoga). But the supreme ideal of the Siddha school, in the North as well as in the South of India, is *freedom, perfect health*, and *immortality—all gained in this life.*

One of the essential points of the new tantric Siddha 'revelation' is that it finally completes the synthesis among the various elements of Buddhist Vajrayāna, Hindu Śaivite tantrism, magic, alchemy, and Haṭha Yoga. According to Eliade (*op. cit.* 304), this synthesis occurred probably first between the 7th–11th Centuries A.D. However, it contained much, much older elements; and it has had a lasting effect: in the Indian South, it lives until this day.

Siddhism was in many ways just a continuation of the tantric synthesis; but it put more emphasis on the value of magic and Yoga as basic means 'for the conquest of freedom and immortality'.

(2) Now we can ultimately approach the specific features of the *Tamil* Siddha school. South Indian, Tamil Siddhism has all the basic components and features common with the North Indian tantric Siddha Yoga: the quest of perfect health and immortality in this life, and hence a preoccupation with *medicine* and *alchemy*; the basic *Haṭha Yoga techniques*; the development of occult powers, the *siddhis*. However, in addition to this complex of fundamental features, the Tamil Siddha movement has some additional components, which are either absent or weak in North Indian Siddhism: the *religious* component of anti-

ritualism and anti-ceremonialism, as well as a suppression of 'devotion' (*bhakti*) in favour of the stress on ethical principles and quest for knowledge; the *philosophical* component which is stronger in some personalities and weaker in others, and which may be captured under the three headings of 'relativism', 'pessimism' and 'disgust'; finally, a very important *social* component, expressed in a pronounced social radicalism and negativism, and, with some Siddhas, in anti-brahminism.

The next seven chapters will discuss the general as well as the specific features and components of the Tamil Siddha movement.

4 *Siddha Medicine*

Siddha medicine will be discussed very briefly. It belongs here only marginally, since this monograph's chief aim is to analyse some Siddha *poets*, not the system of medicine in Tamilnadu which goes under the name of *cittavaittiyam*. Also, the present author is not competent enough to deal with the subject in any appreciable detail.[28]

Sanctity can be achieved only in a divine body. The pessimism and asceticism of the Upaniṣadic and post-Upaniṣadic period give way to a positive attitude towards one's body. The body is no longer a source of pain and temptation, but the most reliable and effective instrument of man in his quest to conquer death and bondage. Since liberation can be gained even in this life, the body must be preserved as long as possible, and in perfect condition, as an aid to meditation leading to freedom.

Because spiritual development is much slower than physical, the ageing of the body must be delayed, so that maturity of body and mind may be enjoyed simultaneously. For achieving full development, the Siddha must hold back time; and he claims he knows how to do it.

The classical attitude of Haṭha Yoga and Siddhism towards the human body is beautifully and clearly expressed in Tirumūlar's *Tirumantiram*. In this marvellous text, the body is valued as the temple of God[29] and as a fit instrument for the soul in its pursuit of self-discipline and search of God (st. 307, 724).

In later Tamil *cittar* texts, however, the body becomes again a matter of abhorrence and disgust, and it seems that these later authors repeat what had been the attitude of the Yoga of Patañjali: physical purification produced the feeling of disgust with one's own body, and cessation of contact with other bodies.[30]

This negative attitude to one's body was, indeed, only a passing phase in the development of Tamil Siddha thought; one may almost say a deviation (most explicitly expressed in Paṭṭiṉattār's songs). It came and it went, and nowadays, in the living *cittar* tradition of the South of India, the attitude towards the body is entirely and fully positive, 'Tirumūlar-like', classically Haṭha-Yogic. According to my Siddha informant, fifty-five years of age is the true prime of life; whereas old age as we in the West know it need not come at all to one who has learned how to arrest physiological age and even, to some extent, to reverse it.

The Siddha medical system claims to be original, not derived from the ancient Ayurvedic system of medicine. Contrary to the Ayurvedic medicinal practice which seems to have been concerned in its therapy primarily with herbs and other organic drugs, the Siddha system, though not adverse to herbs,[31] makes much use of salts, metals, mineral poisons, in short, of anorganic remedies. Sometimes it is said that the three basic methods of Siddha medicine are *maṇi*, *mantiram* and *maruntu*, that is, astrology, reciting *mantras*, and using drugs. According to some modern exponents of Siddha medicine, the Siddha therapy consists of (1) Yoga *āsanas*, *mudrās* and *bandhas*, that is, postures, gestures and 'locks', (2) *cūryacikiccai* or 'sun-baths' and (3) taking drugs (*maruntu*).

The Siddha medical system is said to have been founded by Akattiyar (Sanskrit Agastya)[32] who is credited with having performed the trephination of the skull on his pupil Tēraiyar, removing a toad (*tērai*) from his brain (hence the disciple's name). More than 200 medical treatises are ascribed to Akattiyar; these texts seem to be rather late. The remedies, which are prescribed in them, are both vegetable and chemical. Akattiyar makes a clear distinction between diagnosis and prognosis; he performs a minute examination of the pulse. Some of the medical works contain fascinating details: thus for instance Akattiyar's *Kurunāṭiccūttiram* mentions seminal animalcules, discovered in Western medicine by Ludwig Hamm in 1677.[33]

According to a legend, Auvaiyār, in the times of Akattiyar, had two sons, Irāmatevar[34] and Yākkopu (obviously Yākūb, Jacob), who were the true initiators of the Tamil system of medicine and sorcery. My own Tamil Siddha informant denoted himself as a spiritual descendant of the line of Yākkopu.

According to this informant, there are eighteen Yoga *āsanas* (Tamil *ātaṉam, irukkai*) indispensable for Siddha therapeutic purposes: (1) salutation (*vaṇakkam*), (2) sun-worship (*sūryanamaskāram*), (3) shoulder integral posture (*carvaṅkācaṉam*), (4) fish (*mīn*), (5) crane (*kokku*), (6) bow (*vil*), (7) topsy-turvy posture (*viparītācaṉam*), (8) half-fish (*pātimīṉ*), (9) plough (*kalappai*), (10) serpent (*pāmpu*), (11) yogic symbol pose (*yōkamutrācaṉam*), (12) half-wheel (*pāticakkaram*), (13) sitting crane (*amarnta kokku*), (14) locust (*viṭṭil*), (15) supine pose (*vajroli mutrācaṉam*), (16) kneeling pose (*supta vajrācaṉam*), (17) triangular pose (*mukkōṇācaṉam*), (18) corpse (*cavācaṉam*).[35]

Breathing is of course the most important part of *cittar* therapy. Breath, *pirāṇam*, is the vital energy, and death, *maraṇam*, is defined by Rōma Ṛṣi, one of the classical Siddha therapists, as complete loss of *prāṇa*.[36] On various techniques of breathing, the Siddhas based their theory and practice aiming at physical longevity and, so they claimed, even immortality. According to *Rōma riṣi ñāṉam* 13, a man who is one hundred years old breathes 21,600 times per day. That is, during one hour this healthy centenarian breathes 900 times which will give 15 respirations per minute.[37] The span of life is inversely proportional to the rate of breathing. If the respiration is

15/min. and the length of life 100 years, then 18/min. respirations give us approximately $83\frac{1}{3}$ years. In contrast, the respiration 2/min. gives us $100 \times 15:2 = 750$ years, the respiration 1/min. = 1500 years, and if the respiration is 0/min., the span of life is $100 \times 15:0 = \infty$, that is, *infinity*. If there is no respiration, or rather stoppage, arrest of breath, as in the so-called *corūpa camāti*, the yogin attains immortality, since the span of his life is infinity. Practical consequences, arising out of this somewhat unbelievable argumentation, and appearing in Siddha therapy, sound rather convincing, though: Control your breathing; unnecessary talk, slip-shod panting and gasping, unnecessary respiratory muscle work, all these are harmful.[38] This is the most important 'message' of Yoga: to control breath is to control life itself.

My own Siddha informant practiced in a small dispensary in Mylapore, Madras. It seemed to me that the drugs he used were, with a few exceptions, exclusively anorganic in nature. Apart from drugs (*maruntu*), he prescribed to his patients gentle and simple breathing exercises,[39] and combinations of not very straining *āsanas*.[40] He certainly cured me of a severe digestive and intestinal complaint where Western-type medicine was most unsuccessful.

In the 18th Century (1732), François Bernier, the Montpellier doctor and physician, described, in his *Voyages*, the Indian Siddhas in the following passage: '. . . they are almost constantly travelling hither and thither; they are men who scoff at everything, who take no care for anything; men possessing secrets, and who, the people say, even know how to make gold and to prepare mercury so admirably, that one or two grains taken in the morning restore the body to perfect health and so fortify the stomach that it digests very well and can hardly be satisfied.'[41] I do not know what I was given to swallow by my Siddha physician (he would not tell) in Madras in January 1968, but he did indeed restore my body to 'perfect' health when it was in a rather poor shape.

5 Alchemy

The Siddha preoccupation with *racavātam* or alchemy cannot be dealt with in any detail here, for the same reasons for which Tamil *cittavaittiyam* (medicine) was described only marginally. It is, however, worth while to pause and ask the inevitable question: why alchemy at all? Why the preoccupation of the Siddhas with the transmutation of metals into gold?

First, because 'gold is immortality,'[42] because it is *the* perfect metal, its symbolism equals the symbolism of spiritual perfection, spiritual freedom and autonomy.

As M. Eliade[43] rightly stresses, in this kind of Siddha alchemy we have no prechemistry, no pre-science, but a spiritual technique, operating on matter but seeking above all to bring about deliverance and autonomy of spirit.

Second: the Yogic processes take part in the 'subtle body' (in Tamil terminology *nuṇṇuṭal*), not in the 'gross' physical body (*paruvuṭal*), and this 'subtle' body is made homogenous with the cosmos. The disciple is required to contemplate the creation and dissolution of the cosmos; the recreation of his own 'subtle' body as well as the cosmos. This concentration on one's 'subtle' body as 'cosmicized' leads to the preoccupation with the transformation of 'substance' (*carakku*), with alchemy. We also know of attempts to transmute the body into an incorruptible substance by means of *rasapāna*, an elixir composed mainly of mercury and mica, which symbolized

Śiva and Gaurī, with which the Siddha alchemist identifies himself. Such transsubstantiation helps the yogin to preserve the body in the state of incorruptible health. This information is given by Mādhava in his exposé of different doctrines (*Sarvadarśanasaṃgraha*, 14th Century), under the title *raseśvara-darśana* or 'system of mercury'.

Another point of contact between Siddha Yoga and alchemy: both oppose the purely speculative methods, the purely metaphysical and discursive knowledge; both are empirical, experimental, 'practical', working with concrete techniques. Just as the *cittar* work on their body, so they also work on matter—to finish it, to make it mature, perfect (like their body), to change it into gold, the perfect 'solar' metal. There is thus an occult correspondence between matter and man's psychophysical body.

However, in the *poetry* of the Tamil Siddhar, there is not much about alchemy. Here and there, the poets maintain that they are able to transmute base metals (such as copper) into gold; here and there, they use metaphors and images which have an 'alchemical' character (speaking about transmutation of the Spirit, using the symbols of iron, silver, gold). But most of the alchemical matter is naturally discussed in the very superficially and badly known prosaic treatises ascribed to various Tamil Siddhas—a body of texts which is of no direct concern to us in this book.[44]

6 *Yoga*

This somewhat lengthy chapter is emphatically not a systematic treatise of Haṭha Yoga or any other kind of Yoga. First of all, the author is not at all competent to deal with Yoga as an expert, and he has no wish whatsoever to add to the innumerable vulgarizations which have been written and published about Yoga. More importantly, the main objective of this book is not to deal with Yoga as such but with the Tamil Siddha poets. Hence, Yoga will be treated, in what follows, only as much as it forms an integral part of the ideologies pertinent to the literary works of the Tamil Siddhas, and a necessary pre-requisite for the understanding of their works. A basic acquaintance with tantric oriented Haṭha Yoga is required for anyone who wants to understand correctly most of the poetic texts of the Tamil Siddha poets proper as well as of their 'Siddha-like' forerunners and heirs, since all of them were undoubtedly practising yogins. Hence the necessity for this chapter; however, the reader must always bear in mind that this chapter is neither a systematic exposé of Yoga doctrines nor a practical 'guide' to Yoga techniques.

6.1. There are three principal levels of human constitution which are referred to in the systems of Yoga:

(a) The *spiritual* level, constituted in man by the pure Consciousness itself,[45] which, through Illusion (*māyā*), is individualized in each of us but, in fact, is identical with the Highest Being and with the Universal Life.

(b) This consciousness, which is an *energy*, is expressed in the normal man on the next, *psychological* level with its two familiar subdivisions, the *affective* and the *intellectual*.

(c) Finally, there is the *physiological* level.

Yoga has thus a triadic conception of functional levels in man. The Realization means, in short, to do away with the illusion that Consciousness itself is identical with intellectual and/or affective activity; and the technique to arrive at the realization is, briefly, to suppress the fluctuations of mental activity. This technique of meditation is called *saṃyama*, and has three stages: *dhāraṇā* 'concentration', *dhyāna* 'meditation (in the narrower sense)' and *samādhi* 'union'. The meditative stage should in most, but not all, cases be preceded by Haṭha Yoga, a physiological preparation, consisting of postures (*āsana*), gestures (*mudrā*), contractions or 'locks' (*bandha*) and controlled breathing (*prāṇāyama*).

This, *in nuce*, is what is common to every system of Yoga, including the tantric-oriented Siddha Yoga.

Why is Haṭha Yoga so important? Because the tantric realization, apart from requiring practice (*abhyāsa*, Tamil *appiyācam*), requires a seat of praxis: *the body*. The result of the practice should be the reversal of the process of phenomenalization; and the body must be the arena of this reversal. Only through body bliss is manifested, since only through body phenomenalization is caused.

Tirumūlar, the foremost exponent of Yoga in Tamil, just like the Buddhist tantric yogin Saraha, sees the body as a blissful and sacred place (see below). Says Saraha: 'I have not seen another sacred place as blissful as (my own) body!' And this is the very characteristic approach of all the 'true' earlier Tamil Siddhas, like Tirumūlar or Civavākkiyar. 'If body is destroyed, soul is destroyed', says Tirumūlar. Hence the obsession of the Siddhas with the dream of eternal youth and splendid health.

The Siddhas professed that there was no incurable disease; and that it was possible to maintain eternal youth. It was possible, according to them, to overcome the five limitations of *narai* 'grey hair', *tirai* 'dim vision', *mūppu* 'old age', *nōy* 'disease', and *maraṇam* 'death'. Rāma Ṛṣi says explicitly in *Ñāṉam* 12: 'If you ask what is the sign of true liberation of body and spirit, it is the physical body (*tūla tēkam*) aglow with the fire (of immortality).'

Truth, for the Siddhas, was not interesting and precious in itself. It became valuable by virtue of its soteriological function: because knowledge of truth helps man to liberate himself; and liberation, conquest of absolute freedom, rebirth to a non-conditioned mode of being—that was the supreme end to achieve. This end could be achieved by an ascetic technique and a method of meditation—in short, by Yoga. In this sense, the Tamil Siddhas are all of them yogins. Yet in another sense: as Eliade says, what characterizes Yoga is not only this practical side, but also its initiatory structure. One does not learn Yoga by oneself; the guidance of a master, a *guru*, is absolutely necessary. This is perfectly true of the *cittar*: their teachings, too, must be learned from masters, and are thus initiations, and this transfer of knowledge goes on traditionally from generation to generation (*paraṃparā*, Tamil *paramparaiyāka*). Thus, for instance, my Siddha informant insisted that he belonged to the line of Yākkopu (Yākūb) who was one of the two initiators of the Tamil Siddha medicine.

6.2. The hierarchic and subtile physiology of Haṭha Yoga presupposes a sublime, subtle anatomy. It is extremely important to remember that, according to Yoga, there is a threefold human structure: the Self, the 'subtle' body, and the 'gross' body. The subtle body plays the role of a connection between the gross physical body and the Spirit. There are *correspondences* between the subtle and the physical body, but *not identity*. In addition, and apart from, the gross physical body directly accessible to our senses, with its vertebral column and spinal cord, its arteries, nerves, muscles and so on, there exists, according to Yoga, *another subtle body*, with its own nerves and arteries etc.[46] When a yogin, for instance, meditates on a particular vortex of psychic energy (*cakra*), he does *not* meditate on an anatomic localization in his physical body which would correspond to a subtle centre (*cakra*), but on that subtle centre itself.

Thus, the 'veins', 'nerves', 'centres' and so on of Yoga do *not* designate actual anatomical organs and strictly physiological function 'on the surface', directly accessible to our sensory perception. Corresponding no doubt to actual psychosomatic experience, related to the 'deep structure' of human life, they are 'transphysiological'. The body that serves as a primary vehicle is the actual 'gross' material body of the yogin. But he becomes, subsequently, master of the 'subtle body', 'of a zone infinitely greater than the "normal" psychic zone' (Eliade). The basic point of departure, as stressed above, is the material human body, however; transformed into a microcosmos, or into an anthropocosmos (which is 'realized' through yogic meditation), so that one may speak, as Eliade does, of 'cosmo-physiology'.

Of course, a very intimate relationship—a relationship which is the basis of Haṭha Yoga—exists between the 'gross' physical, material body, and the 'subtle' body, the object of Yogic meditation. Several very serious scientists and scholars have recently investigated the physiological 'powers' obtained by those who practice the genuine, traditional, and unadulterated Haṭha Yoga. These investigators have found, and described (in perfectly sound and serious scientific journals) the astonishing abilities of the yogins to control the neurovegetative system, and to influence decisively their respiratory and cardiac rhythms. They extend the control normally exercised over the striated muscles to the non-striated muscles; and this would explain, for instance, the ability to pump and expel liquids by the urethra (or the rectum) as well as the arrest of seminal emission (and even the 'return of semen').

Dr. Thérèse Brosse—on the basis of experiments with 92 subjects, among them 11 Hindu yogins—has established the physiological authenticity of phenomena which had for a long time been considered impossible or doubtful: cf. the path-breaking work *Etudes expérimentales des techniques du Yoga, Expérimentation psychosomatique* (*Ecole française d'Extrême-Orient*, Paris, 1963).[47]

6.3. The most important component of the 'subtle' body, for the purpose of Yoga techniques, are the *nāḍīs* ('conduits') and the *cakras* ('centres').

The *nāḍīs* ('conduits', 'vessels', 'nerves') are channels of *prāṇic* energy. They form an invisible network of conduits of vital forces. Vital energy, *prāṇa*, which is present in and activating all which lives, circulates in form of 'breaths' through the *nāḍīs*. Where many such 'subtle' conduits meet, a centre or *cakra* exists.

There is an immense number of *nāḍīs*; some texts give the number as 300,000, some as 80,000, most often the number 72,000 is quoted. However, the most important *nāḍīs* used in Yoga techniques, are the first three in the traditional enumeration of ten, namely the *iḍā* (a channel on the left side of the spinal column, terminating in the left nostril), the *piṅgalā* (a channel on the right side of the spinal column, terminating in the right nostril), and the *suṣumṇā* or *brahmanāḍī*, the 'middle way' (corresponding to the spinal column).[48]

On the anatomo-physiological plane, the *iḍā* and *piṅgalā* correspond to the laterovertebral sympatic nerve chains, and the *suṣumṇā* to the spinal cord.

The *cakras* or centres are vortices of psychic energy. As stressed above, they do not 'exist' as such in the 'physical' matter, but may be considered as vital centres, regulators of higher psychic and spiritual forces, which condition all physical responses.[49]

There are seven important *cakras* ('discs', 'wheels', 'centres'), which correspond, in the physical body, to the sympatic plexuses and the *sutura frontalis.* They are also called 'lotuses' because they are 'composed' of constantly whirling streams of energy which radiate outwards in 'petal-like' emanations. The *cakras* are extremely important in Yoga techniques, and hence must be described in some detail here.

(1) The *mūlādhāra* ('root') is situated at the base of the spinal column, between the anal orifice and the genital organs. It corresponds to the pelvic or sacrococcygeal plexus, and to the adrenal glands. It is of the 'substance' of 'earth' (Ta. *maṇ*). It is symbolized by a red lotus inside a circle and/or a triangle with four petals, on which are ascribed in gold the letters *v*, *ś*, *s*, *h*; the triangle with the apex downward is the symbol of *yoni*, the female genital organ. In its centre is the *svayambhūliṅga* ('the *liṅga* existing by itself'), its head brilliant as a ruby. Coiled eight times like a snake around the *liṅga* sleeps the absolute mistress of all the *cakras*, the great universal energy, called Kuṇḍalinī or Kuṇḍalī, blocking the opening of the *liṅga* with her mouth or her head, thus obstructing the access to the *suṣumṇā*. This *cakra* is related to the cohesive power of matter, to inertia. The Siddha sources give a summary of points to remember when meditating on this *cakra*: (1) coiled Kuṇḍalī, (2) triangle, (3) four-petaled lotus, (4) ruby-colour, (5) god Gaṇapati, (6) the sound *oṁ*. Or, very briefly: 'It is necessary to meditate on it as on golden light and four-petaled red lotus.'

(2) The *svādiṣṭhāna cakra*, also called *jalamaṇḍala* ('water-circle') and *meḍhrādhāra* (*meḍhra*= penis) is situated 'two-fingers-breadths' above the first *cakra* in the lumbar region at the base of the male genital organ. It corresponds to the sacral plexus, and the sex glands. It is symbolized by a lotus within a square with six vermilion petals inscribed with the letters *b*, *bh*, *m*, *y*, *r*, *l*. According to some authorities, its element is water, according to others, fire. In the middle of the lotus there is a white half-moon, and in its centre the letter *n*, inside which sits

Brahma with Sarasvatī. It is related to white colour, the *prāṇa* breath and the sense of taste. Points for meditation: (1) square, (2) six-petaled vermilion lotus, (3) fire-like red colour, (4) diamond-like white glow, (5) god Brahma and goddess Sarasvatī, (6) the sound *na*.

(3) The *maṇipura* ('jewelled city') or *nābhiṣṭhāna* ('umbilicus') is situated 'eight-fingers-breadths' above the 2nd *cakra*, in the region of the solar plexus at the level of the navel, and corresponds to the epigastric plexus and the pancreas gland. According to Tamil sources, it is the *untikamalam* ('the lotus of the navel'), the source of the breath which produces all sounds including human speech. It is symbolized by a circle with ten-petaled blue lotus and the letters *ḍ, ḍh, ṇ, t, th, d, dh, n, p, ph* inscribed on the petals. Inside the lotus is the letter *m*. According to some descriptions, a big snake lies inside with Mahāviṣṇu and Mahālakṣmī, and the *cakra* is related to water. According to others, it is related to fire, sun and *rajas* (menstrual fluid), and the sense of sight. Points for meditation: (1) Ten-petaled lotus, (2) emerald or blue colour, (3) god Viṣṇu and goddess Lakṣmī, (4) the letter and sound *ma*.

(4) The *anāhata cakra*, situated ten finger-breadths above the third centre, in the cardiac plexus, and corresponding to the thymus, shines like a rising sun, its element being air; it is the true seat of *prāṇa* and of *jīvātman*, the Self; it is called 'the lotus of the heart'. It is symbolized by a triangle with a red lotus with twelve golden petals, inscribed by the letters *k, kh, g, gh, n, c, ch, j, jh, ñ, ṭ, ṭh*. In the middle are two interlaced triangles, in the centre of them another golden triangle shining like sun, with a *liṅga* and the letter *śi*. God Śiva (Rudra) or Īśvara (the personal Lord) with Pārvatī Śakti, red in colour, sits inside. The centre is related to the sense of touch, to the phallus, to the blood-vessel system and to motoric force. Points for meditation: (1) Twelve-petaled lotus, (2) triangle, (3) crystal colour, (4) god Rudra and goddess Pārvatī, (5) the letter *śi*.

(6) The *viśuddha cakra* ('the wheel of purity') is situated in the

region of the throat at the junction of the spinal column and the *medulla oblongata*; it corresponds to the laryngeal–pharyngeal plexus and the thyroid gland. It is symbolized by a hexagon (two triangles forming 'Solomon's seal'), inside which is a sixteen-petaled lotus the colour of which is smoky purple (Tamil *mēkam*). Within the lotus is a blue area with a white circle containing an elephant, and on the elephant is the *bīja-mantra haṅg*, supporting androgynous Sadāśiva who is half silver, half golden. Or, according to other sources, inside the lotus is the letter *v*, supporting Maheśvara and Maheśvarī. This *cakra* is related to white colour and its substance is ether (*ākāśa*). Points for meditation: (1) Hexagon, (2) sixteen-petaled lotus, (3) smoky colour, (4) god Maheśvara and goddess Maheśvarī, (5) the letter *v*.

(6) The *ājñācakra* (in Tamil sources *ākñēyam*), the centre of 'command', is situated between the eyebrows 'like the lamp of knowledge', and corresponds to the craneal plexus and the pituitary and pineal glands. It is the seat of cognitive faculties, of mind, intelligence, the 'Ich-Gefühl', and of the senses, in their 'subtle' modality. It is symbolized by a two-petaled or a three-petaled lotus, white in colour; inside is a white triangle, the symbol of *yoni*, in the middle of which is a white *liṅga*, the seat of Sadāśiva or Paramaśiva and his *śakti* Manonmaṇi. Also, the sound *y* is inside, and the *mantra* is *oṁ*. Points for meditation: (1) Three-petaled lotus in a semicircle, (2) crystal colour, (3) god Sadāśiva and goddess Manonmaṇi, (4) the letter *y*.

(7) The *sahasrāra cakra* is situated, according to some authorities, at the top of the head, corresponding to the pituitary and pineal glands in the cerebrum; however, more traditional authorities say that this *cakra* does not belong any more to the physical or even to the 'subtle' body, but is 'above' it, symbolizing the plane of transcendence. It is also called *brahmārandhra* or *nirvāṇa-cakra*. It is represented by a thousand-petaled lotus, head down, and the petals bear all possible combinations of the Sanskrit alphabet. In the middle is a full moon enclosing a triangle:

here, the final union of Śiva and Śakti, the final goal of tantric meditation is realized, and here the Kuṇḍalinī ends her journey.

The doctrine of the six *ādhāras* or the seven *cakras* is so very important because all Yoga techniques, and especially their tantric varieties, ultimately aim at the 'opening' of the Kuṇḍalinī, the master energy, and her passage through the *cakras*. But, according to some later Tamil sources, even without the arousing of the Kuṇḍalī, the *prāṇa* in the form of 'breath' moves through the *cakras* and awakens the gods. First, between 6–6.40 in the morning, by breathing 600 times, Gaṇapati is aroused and 'his hunger satisfied'; in the next *cakra*, between 6.41–13.20 hours, by breathing 6000 times, god Brahma-Prajāpati is 'satisfied'; in the third *cakra* (umbilical), Mahāviṣṇu 'feeds' on our 6000 breaths between 13.20–20.00 hours; in the 'lotus of the heart', Rudra is fed by 6000 breaths between 20.01–2.40 hours; in the pharyngeal region, Maheśvara 'feeds' on our 1000 breaths between 2.41–3.46 hours. Then, in the region of the eyebrows, we satisfy by another 1000 breaths Īśvara or Paramaśiva (between 3.47 and 4.53 hours). And in the *sahasrāra cakra*, Paramātmā is satisfied by another 1000 breaths between 4.54–6.00 hours. Thus, everyone's body is a pantheon, each region having its deity. And more than that: the body is transformed into a microcosm; the disciple identifies himself with the Cosmos, rediscovering the genesis and the destruction of the universe in our own body.

In its more subtle and sophisticated form, the identification of one's own body with the universe is present even in such philosophical thought as that of Śrī Ramaṇa Mahāṛṣi. Cf. e.g. dialogue 616 (January 1939) in *Talks with Sri Ramana Maharsi* (4th ed., 1968, 578): 'The entire Universe is condensed in the body, and the entire body in the Heart. Thus the Heart is the nucleus of the whole Universe.' And 'This concentration is called *samyamana* in the Yoga *Sastras*. . . . Even worlds can be created in this manner. *Samyamana* leads to all *siddhis*.'

The main yogic goal, however, is, as pointed out above,

the awakening of the Kuṇḍalī and her ascent through the *cakra* to the 'Thousand-petaled Lotus'.

6.4. Kuṇḍalinī or Kuṇḍalī is the great universal power (*śakti*), the absolute mistress of all *cakras* existing potentially in all of them.[50]

She moves in the *suṣumṇā* channel, by the force aroused in the inner sense (*manas*) by manipulating the *prāṇa*; she is awakened by *āsanas* (postures), controlled breathing, and concentration on the centres. She is a 'goddess'—Śakti, Īśvarī, Arundhatī—identified also with the mantra *oṁ*, and possessive of all the attributes of all gods and all goddesses. Normally, however, in each of us, she dwells or 'sleeps' lying coiled like a snake at the base of the spine.

The awakening of Kuṇḍalinī, which should be practiced only after long preparation and under expert supervision, arouses intense heat, and her progress through the *cakras* is manifested by the lower part of the body being inert and cold like a corpse, while the part through which she passes is burning hot. This awakening of the Kuṇḍalinī is only the beginning; the yogin then tries to keep the power in the median duct (*suṣumṇā*), and to make it reach the top *cakra*. When this happens, the yogin attains what is called *layayoga samādhi*, an immersion into blissful state (a kind of *nirvikalpa samādhi*), often accompanied by the acquisition of miraculous powers (*siddhi*). However, this effort, according to *tāntrik* texts, is seldom successful. To hasten the ascent of the Kuṇḍalī, some *tāntrik* schools combined corporeal postures and breathing with sexual practices, the underlying idea being the necessity of achieving simultaneous arrestation of breath, thought and sperm. This brings us to the discussion of tantric eroticism as far as it is needed for the understanding of Tamil Siddha texts.

6.5. The ultimate reason for the opinion that union with God can be achieved also (or only!) through sexual union, is the fundamental metaphysical principle that the Absolute Reality is *advaya*, that is, *non-dual*, that it contains all dualities and polarities; and that the creation, the becoming, represents the destruction of this primordial Unity, and the separation of two principles. Hence man, experiencing a state of duality, suffers, since this experience *is illusion*, bondage, suffering. To remove this suffering and to destroy this illusion, one has to *realize* the unity; one has to *act*, in conformity with the esoteric doctrine, transmitted from mouth to ear and from generation to generation. One kind of realization of the primordial unity, one kind of *action* is the *sexual union.*

Tirumūlar, in his *Tirumantiram* 813, states *in nuce* the basic properties of this tantric sexual union:

'The age reached [by the woman should be at least] twenty and [that by the man at least thirty]. The woman with rich tresses, and the splendid man, who are [sexually] united, experience highest pleasure. The *citta* ("mind, consciousness, intellect") has blossomed and spread and dissolved [in bliss] after [the man] attained union with the woman. But the semen will not trickle and wither.'

Sexuality is ritual; this fact is the key to the understanding of all tantric and Siddha sexuality, even of the seeming obscenities of the language of the texts in question. That is: the sexual plane is sanctified and homogenized with myth and ritual; and, vice versa, the ritual and the myth may be and often is explained in sexual terms.

The concept is pan-Indian and very ancient. Thus for instance the very old text of *Aitareya Brāhmaṇa* X, 3, 2–4 says: 'If, in the course of a recitation, the priest separates the first two quarters of a verse and brings the other two close together, this is because the woman separates her thighs and the man presses them during pairing; the priest thus represents pairing, so that the sacrifice will give a numerous progeny.'

In Tamil Siddha texts, we have, occasionally, sexual imagery and symbolism. From prehistoric times, the sphere of sex and the sphere of religion have been intimately connected, almost in any culture, and specifically in India, which has known countless rites implying sexuality.

More specifically, in tantric thinking, and in some Tamil Siddha texts, every naked woman incarnates *prakṛti*, 'nature'. Hence she is to be looked upon with the same awe and adoration that one feels when thinking about the secrets of nature and its creativity. One may even speak of 'ritual nudity'. Further, this woman-nature should be transformed into an incarnation of Śakti; the woman becomes the Goddess, the yogin incarnates Śiva; their 'rite', their ritual copulation, *is* the copulation of the divine couple. The sex act is not a profane act, but a rite, the partners are no longer human beings but gods, sexual union becomes the union of opposites. The arresting of the flow of the sperm, like the immobilization of respiration and the suspension of thought are the three formulas expressing one of the great paradoxes, destined to conquer our 'historicity': the abolishment of time. For the sexual act, if it indeed is a *tāntrik* act, *must never terminate in the emission of sperm*. The Sanskrit texts say again and again: *bodhicittam notsṛjet* 'the semen must not be emitted'. Otherwise the yogin falls under the laws of time and death. Cf. e.g. what Tirumūlar has to say about this in *Tirumantiram* 814.1: *veḷḷiyuruki poṉvaḻi ōṭāmē* 'the silver (= sperm) must not flow the way of gold (= vulva)'. Those who let the semen flow through the 'tube' (*kuḻal*= penis), are called 'false silversmiths' (= false, pretentious yogins).

Why then ritual cohabitation at all? One of the reasons is no doubt that the sensual pleasure producing maximum tension abolishes normal consciousness and inaugurates the *samarasa*, the nirvāṇic state which is obtained by arresting breath, thought, and sperm. Another reason is the identification of the sexual partners with Śiva and Śakti, and the esoteric meaning of their sexual act as the union of opposites.

Before I close the discussion of the matter of sex in Siddha

Yoga, let me give a brief instruction how to perform the arresting of the sperm according to my Siddha informant: When the sperm is about to flow, one should seize the penis with the middle fingers of the left hand at its root in front of the anus and pressing hard, expel slowly his breath through the nose, at the same time performing contractions of the anal muscles in the *aśvinīmudrā* or *mūlabandha*,[51] drawing them inward and upward.

6.6. The first step in the physical technique of Haṭha Yoga are the postures or *āsanas* (Tamil *ācaṉam*, *ātaṉam*, *irukkai*) which play an important role as the very basis of Yogic physiological practice. According to *Yogadarśana* II, 46, an *āsana* is the ability 'to rest immobile for a long time and without effort'. Obviously it is necessary to distinguish between postures which do not have but a purely physical function (i.e. either *āsanas* as parts of a physical culture, or therapeutic *āsanas*, used in the Siddha medical system), and the meditative postures.

The term *āsana* itself does not occur too early in the textual evidence. It does not appear in the earliest Upaniṣads, being first mentioned only in *Śvetāśvatara Up.* II, 10; but it occurs in the *Bhagavadgītā*. The practice, however, is undoubtedly archaic (cf. seals found at Mohenjo Daro, Vedic texts referring to yogic postures). The Haṭha-yogic *Gheraṇḍasaṃhitā* enumerates 32 postures; *Haṭhayogapradīpikā* only 15 postures; but *Śivasaṃhitā* as many as 84 postures.

The postures have not only therapeutic value, or the value of the means how to 'immobilize' the body for concentration and meditation; for tantric and Siddha Yoga, some postures have positive magical value: for example *padmāsana* ('lotus') cures any kind of illness; *vajrāsana* ('diamond') confers miraculous powers; *bhujaṅgāsana* ('cobra') arouses the Kuṇḍalinī, and so on.

Accompanying the postures are *bandhas* and *mudrās*. *Bandhas* are contractions pertaining to isolated muscles or to groups of muscles. E.g. *uḍḍīyanabandha* concerns the elevation of the diaphragm by contracting abdominal muscles and plays an important role in the yogic 'stoppage of heart'. Or the *mūla-bandha*, 'anal contraction' of the anal sphincters is used when arresting the flow of sperm.

The *mudrās* or 'gestures' are often accompanied by *mantras*, oral formulas of great magic power, and are performed in certain postures. A few *mudrās* are of cardinal importance. Thus for example the *khecarīmudrā*, the arresting of expiration by the tongue, preceding by forceful inspiration, used for the stoppage of breath; or the *yonimudrā*, which is one of the most effective techniques for shutting off the human organism to sensoric impressions by closing the ears with thumbs, the eyes with index fingers, the nostrils with middle fingers, and the upper and lower lips with the remaining two fingers, concentrating, at the same time, on a light behind the eyes and repeating the mantra *ham* (inspiration) and *sa* (expiration).

6.7. The next step in Yoga discipline, after the postures, is controlled breathing or *prāṇāyama*. For the yogin, the only Reality is Pure Consciousness, and this Reality is concrete and dynamic: an energy, on which rests the cosmic and the human systems. The vital energy, *prāṇa*, is a manifestation of the Cosmic Consciousness; all which lives is maintained by *prāṇa*, the cosmic breath, the expiration of Brahmaṇ. Hence, the entire human life, its complete functional dynamism, somatic, mental, and spiritual, rests on *prāṇa*. Man is an individualization of the same life which, in the cosmos, is the elementary life-energy. The aim of Yoga is to do away with the dualism and return to the unity. On each of the three levels mentioned above, the yogin tries to gain the mastery of *prāṇa*. In *prāṇa*, the universal and divine vital energy, individualized in man on the three levels, resides, too, the essence of human functional unity. *Prāṇa* is thus not just respiratory breath. It is a vital force which moves not only the human and animal bodies, but the entire universe; in the human body, all movement is also commanded by the inner circulation of this energy.[52] Now *prāṇāyama*, the breathing technique, is, naturally, a physical technique, which has a number of stages. During the first stage, heavy perspiration appears; during the second stage, the yogin trembles violently; during the third, he 'hops about like a frog' (*Gheraṇḍa Saṃhitā* V); during the fourth, he rises into air. According to Theos Bernard's personal experience,[53] all these stages except the last correspond to what he actually did undergo.

However, the true, 'higher' *prāṇāyama* symbolizes and equates, in the phase of expiration, the destruction of the illusion that the objective is real; in the phase of inspiration, the acquirement of the certitude of 'I am Brahmaṇ'; in arresting the breath, the concentration on that certitude. Under this form, controlled breathing and meditation become identical.

According to Śrī Ramaṇa Mahārṣi, undoubtedly one of the very genuine exponents of classical Yoga, the yogic *prāṇāyama* is a necessary step to be practiced during the period of training; the yogic control of *prāṇa* is one of the true principal means for the 'destruction of mind', that is of discursive, intellectual knowledge. The mind gets first controlled by regulation of breath or by its absolute retention. *Prāṇāyama* or controlled breathing, consisting of exhaling the vital air (*recaka*), inhaling it (*pūraka*) and retaining it 'in the heart' (*kumbhaka*)[54] should be practiced daily, according to the adept's ability, slowly and gradually. Such practice will lead to a desire in the mind 'to rest in bliss without moving'. In that moment, one should start practising the *pratyahāra* which Śrī Ramaṇa explains as 'preventing name and form, which had been removed, from re-entering the mind'. Elsewhere, he explains the outcome of *recaka* (exhalation) as 'removing the unreal of name and form from objects constituting the world', of *pūraka* (inhalation) as 'grasping the three real aspects—existence (*sat*), consciousness (*cit*) and bliss (*ānanda*)', and of *kumbhaka* (arrest of breath) as 'retaining the aspects thus grasped'.

Elsewhere, however, Śrī Ramaṇa stresses again and again that breath-control is only an aid 'for diving inwards. One can as well dive down by controlling the mind. On the mind being controlled the breath is automatically controlled. . . . Breath control is recommended for the person who cannot control his mind directly. For those who can control their mind and concentrate, it is not necessary. It can be used at the beginning until one is able to control the mind but then it should be given up. . . . It is one of the various methods that are intended to help one attain *ekagratha* or "one-pointedness" of the mind.'

That there exists a very intimate, and to a great extent still somewhat 'mysterious' connection between controlled breathing and 'mind control' and other psychosomatic phenomena has been established beyond doubt by the experiments conducted by Dr. Brosse.[55] As stressed above, it may be one of the greatest contributions of Yoga to the modern investigation of deep biological and psychosomatic secrets of man that it has made us aware of the extraordinary importance of the 'mystery of respiration'.

6.8. Since Vedic times, but especially in tantrism, *mantras* or 'magic utterances' and *dhāraṇīs* (lit. 'she who upholds') were raised to a vehicle of salvation. The philosophic importance and the practical value of the *mantras* rests on two facts: first, the yogic function of sounds used as 'supports' for concentration (*dhāraṇā*); second, in the interiorized *tāntrik* liturgy, the 'mystical sound' itself has a specific function, yielding its meaning only to the initiated during meditation.

The majority of *mantras* are mutilated or unintelligible words, utterances which, so it would seem, have no 'sense', i.e. sequences of sounds which have no meaning. They have the value of sacred, initiatory language, unintelligible to the uninitiated. They yield their meaning only when uttered in accordance with the rules, and when 'awakened', that is, assimilated during meditation. A classical example is the mantra *a+u+m=oṃ* which, *per se*, as such, has no 'meaning'. However, there are *mantras* which have a 'surface' meaning apart from a deeper mystical meaning, for instance the 'five letters', *na-ma-śi-vā-ya* which means (on the 'surface') 'Obeisance to Śiva'.

The *mantras* have to be received from the master's mouth, and only then they have unlimited power. All *siddhis* may be obtained through the mystical formulas; but the technique of uttering them is not easy; one has first to purify one's thoughts; concentrate on each sound compounding the *mantra*; utter the *mantra* with the most scrupulous precision, and so on.

Each god has a *bīja-mantra*, a 'seed-sound', which is his very being, his very essence. By repeating the *bīja-mantra*, the adept appropriates its ontological essence, assimilates directly and concretely the god. Thus for example in Tamil *cittar* practice, the basic *mantra* is naturally the sacred 'five-letters', cf. Civavākkiyar' stanza 106:

> 'By the true understanding of *ōm namacivāyamē*, and having grasped the Truth,
> by the true understanding of *ōm namacivāyamē* when the Truth shines clear,
> by the true understanding of *ōm namacivāyamē*, and having grasped the Truth
> the ŌMNAMACIVĀYAMĒ rests united with the Self in the Heart!'

For those who know how to utter true *mantras* effectively, there is no death. Cf. Civavākkiyar 364:

> 'There is absolutely no death for those who generate the *mantra* of the rising breath perceiving the essence of *mantras*; for, behold, true *mantras* don't just ooze like the sap from a tree; you are bewildered, men: there *are mantras*!'

The *true mantra* is only one: the *Śivāyam*, and a mere empty repetition of it has no effect; one must indeed understand it truly, *know* it and utter it with *power*, and then it is omnipotent, cf. again Civavākkiyar's stanzas 486 and 22:

> 'The true *mantra* is the one which rests in the Light;
> the *mantra* of Calm has taken shape and become a form;
> the white *mantra* rose and ripened and became sacred Ash,
> for the true *mantra* is only one: *Śivāyame*.'

> 'You were born in the Five Letters. You were raised in the Five Letters!
> You poor people of five elements who chant the Five Letters!
> If only you knew one letter of the Five and uttered it with Power,
> the Lord in the Hall would dance: Fear not! Fear not!'

A *mantra* is a 'symbol' in the archaic sense of the term; a symbolized reality, and a symbolizing sign (Eliade, *op. cit.* 215). There is an occult correspondence between the *mantras*—the mystical sounds (or letters, if the *mantra* was written down), the 'subtle' organs of the human body, and the divine forces manifested in the cosmos. For the cosmos is a vast fabric of magical forces, and these forces can be awakened in the human body by the techniques of mystical physiology (Yoga) which includes the uttering of *mantras*.[56]

There can be hardly any more lofty expression of the immense importance and power of a *mantra* than another Tamil stanza by Civavākkiyar, No. 2:

> 'Within the Five Realized Sounds
> there is the Universe and the Unlimited One
> Within the Five Realized Sounds
> there are the Three Primeval Ones
> Within the Five Realized Sounds
> there is the Beginning and the Illusion of Creation
> Within the Five Realized Sounds
> there is All and Everything.'

6.9. *Maṇḍalas*, like *mantras*, are used as 'support' for meditation. The yogin also uses them as weapons against mental distractions and temptations. The simplest *maṇḍala* is the *yantra*, a diagram 'drawn or engraved on metal, wood, skin, stone, paper, or simply traced on the ground or a wall',[57] e.g. a series of triangles, surrounded by circles, where ▽ equals *yoni*, the female sex-organ, symbol of Śakti, and △ equals *liṅga*, the male sex-organ, symbol of Śiva.

A 'modern' *yantra* is reproduced here (the Tamil 'letters' are *va-ci-na-ma-ya* and stand for the great *mantra civayanama*, that is *śivāya nama*, discussed above).

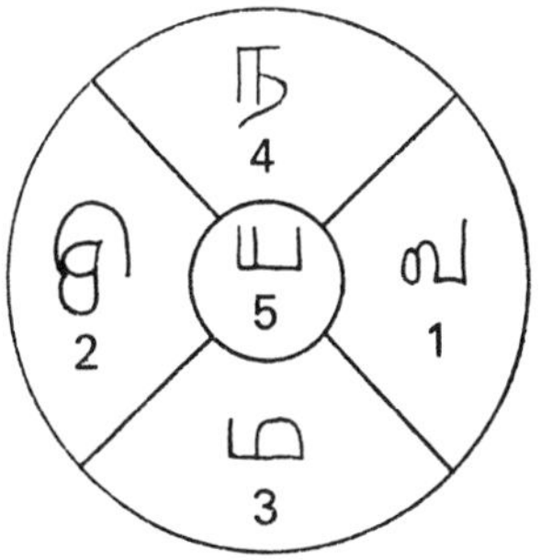

Iconography, too, plays an important part in tantric Yoga; like *mantras*, divine images are 'supports', visual supports in this case, for meditation; but, like *mantras*, they are more than that. One must of course understand the meaning of an icon, the meaning of its symbolism; as a further step, one should visualize a divine image, construct it mentally, 'interiorize' it. Finally, the visualization of a divine image is followed by the identification with the divinity it represents. Now all these steps, in fact, the entire function of icons, seem to be absent from most if not all Tamil Siddha writings. Here is a very important point of difference between other forms of tantric *sādhanā* and the Tamil *cittar* contemplation and meditation. Actually, most if not all Tamil Siddhas have an openly negative, iconoclastic attitude towards idol-worship. Paṭṭiṉattār in IX, 16 sings: 'I cannot exalt the polished stone or the moulded lime or the burnished brass; truly, within my heart I set His two feet similar to gold. . . . Now I do not need anything more.' And Civavākkiyar's st. 34 says:

'In bricks and granite,
in the red-rubbed lingam,
in copper and brass
is Śiva's abode—
that's what you tell us,
and you're wrong.
Stand on your feet
and study yourselves.
Then you will become
the Temple of God,
full of His dance and spell and song.'

6.10. The ultimate goal of Yoga is *saṃyama* which has three successive stages: *dhāraṇā* or mental concentration; *dhyāna* or contemplation; and *samādhi* or 'union'. Of all this, intellectual grasp is not enough. One never can and will understand Yoga completely from outside; it has to 'happen' to one. In our culture, we are all much too 'cerebral'. We have to stop thinking once in a while, and this is precisely the final aim of Yogic *saṃyama*.

Since, however, as stressed earlier, this is not a treatise on Yoga, I shall not deal in any detail with this last stage. Instead, I shall just give as the most basic information and guidance a schematic chart of *samādhi*, the ultimate 'union'. This is fundamentally of two kinds, *nirvikalpa samādhi* or 'union without thoughts' and *salvikalpa samādhi* 'union with thought, with reason' still functioning.

What is important, indeed, most important to realize is the fact that the true yogin, including the Siddha yogin, does not, while experiencing *samādhi*, 'sink' into self-hypnosis, into a

- *samādhi*
  - *nirvikalpa s.*
    - *layayoga sa.* immersion into blissful state, effected by Kuṇḍalinī, often accompanied by acquisition of *siddhis.*
    - *rājayoga s.*
      - *sahaja nirvikalpa samādhi* the permanent *samādhi*, when the mind dissolves in Self: the state of *jīvanmukta*; this is the end of ignorance and captivity, the total deliverance (as achieved in our times e.g. by Ramaṇa Mahārṣi).
      - *kevala nirvikalpa samādhi* a temporary *samādhi*, which is not identical with total and ultimate deliverance.
  - *salvikalpa s.*
    - *mantrayoga s.* the yogin achieves the state of *mahābhava* without speech and motion.
    - *haṭhayoga s.* arrest of respiration and cessation of consciousness of the external world through Haṭha Yoga techniques.

trance, but enters into the various 'states' and stages and kinds of *samādhi* with utmost lucidity: it is not the *sub*consciousness which he seeks but *super*consciousness or *trans*consciousness. Or, in other words, *consciousness of freedom.* This fact may be supported by quotations from all Tamil Siddha texts, beginning with Tirumūlar, and ending with Tāyumāṉavar, Rāmalinga Svāmi and Ramaṇa Mahārṣi. Cf. the following stanza (No. 115) of 'The Siddha with the Dancing Snake':

> 'One must delve deep
> into the Self of the Heart
> and a gentle Fire start;
> and know what means In and Out.

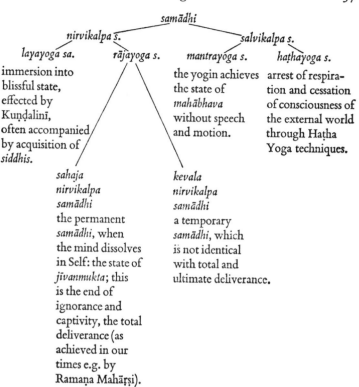

And flowing through the net of streams
beyond false perceptions and dreams
stand firm and gaze above the nose and eyes.

Seeking the Self, Brilliant Supreme Light
I saw, o Snake, the Feet of Bliss and Might!'

In the writings of the Siddhas of Tamilnadu, the three highest roads to liberation—Upaniṣadic *knowledge*, Yogic *technique*, and *devotion-bhakti*, are integrated into one whole, though the greatest stress, with most authors, is ultimately put on the contemplative and psychophysiological techniques destined to gain the knowledge. But the most important, the crucial and central point in the philosophy of the Siddhas is the fact that they understood liberation as *the conquest of immortality in this life*:

'What is the sign of absolute and true liberation?
The physical body aglow with the Fire of Immortality.'
(*Urōma riṣi ñāṉam* 12)

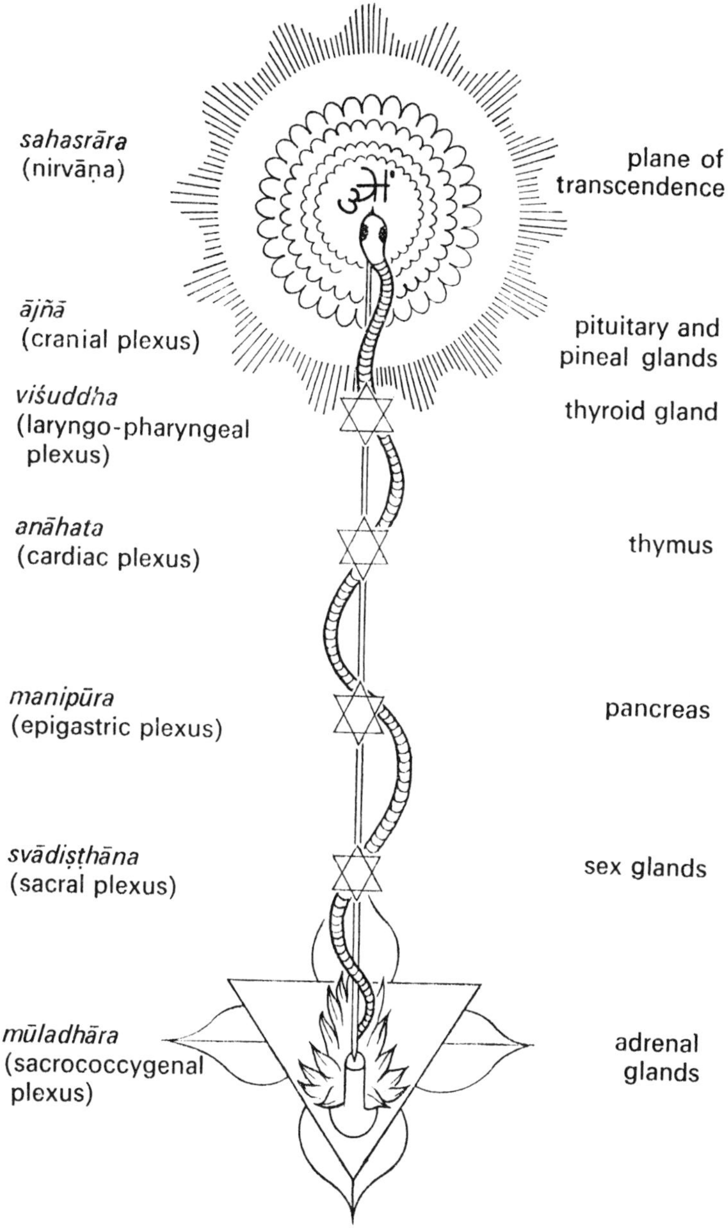

The ascent of Kuṇḍalī through the *cakras*.

7 *The Powers*

A Siddha or Mahāsiddha (Tamil *cittaṉ*, pl. *cittar*) is a yogin who has acquired *siddhi*, that is, 'power, prowess, strength, ability'. From the technique of acquiring such power or powers, and from the description of these powers, it is obvious that the 'power' or 'powers' meant are occult, miraculous, supernatural, magic; that is, extraordinary abilities which normal man, a non-Siddha, does not possess. These miraculous powers are described in Book III of the *Yogasūtras*. Thus Patañjali himself mentions the *siddhi* of *laghiman* (III. 45), that is the power to be so light that one can fly through the air. According to *Mahābhārata* XII, 317, 6, 'with such a body (= yogic body), the yogin goes where he will.'

However, it is the commentaries on the *Yogasūtras*, especially Bhoja's and Vācaspatimitra's commentaries which give a systematic classification of the *siddhis*, and describe the techniques of how to achieve them.

Bhoja in his commentary on *YS* III. 44 quotes eight 'great powers' (*mahāsiddhis*), and these eight reappear again and again until they enter the Tamil *cittar* tradition as well.

(1) *aṇiman* (Tamil *aṇimā*) or 'shrinking' is the faculty of reducing oneself to the size of an atom;

(2) *mahiman* (Tamil *makimā*) or 'illimitability' is the power of increasing one's size without limit and reaching for any object at any distance;

(3) *laghiman* (Tamil *lakimā*) 'lightness' is the power of becoming light as wool and float through the air;

(4) *gariman* (Tamil *karimā*) 'weight' is the power of rendering the body immaterial and to penetrate matter;

(5) *prākāmya* (Tamil *pirakamiyam*) or 'irresistible will', the power to overcome natural obstacles;

(6) *iśitva* (Tamil *icattuvam*) 'supremacy' is the supreme dominion over body and mind, animate and inanimate nature;

(7) *vaśitva* (Tamil *vacittuvam*) 'dominion over the elements' involves the ability to change the course of nature and assuming any form;

(8) *kāmāvasāyitva* (Tamil *pirātti*) 'fulfilment of desires' means the power of attaining everything desired.

There are indeed other 'powers', or an extension of these 'original' eight *mahāsiddhis*; thus the *siddhi* of *lakimā* results in the secret of magical flight, emergence from one's own physical body, 'ascent to the heavens' and so on. There is the power of magical *heat* which is obtained by yogic breathing and transmutation of sexual energy, and accompanied by luminous phenomena. There is the power of entering another's body, of reanimation of corpses, etc., and a specific Indian *siddhi*: the ability to remember previous incarnations.

The Siddha obtains his magical powers by concentrating (*dhāraṇā*), meditating (*dhyāna*) and practicing *samādhi*, *vis-à-vis* a certain object or a class of objects. The yogic technique of *saṃyama* results in a knowledge which is a *possession*. By concentrating and meditating on an object, the Siddha 'assimilates' the object magically, he takes possession of it. First he *concentrates* (*dhāraṇā*) on the object or idea in question. When he has succeeded in having censored absolutely all distractions, and concentrating properly on the one particular object or idea or prowess to be obtained (*ekāgratā*), he meditates (*dhyāna*) the object; this finally results in the *identification* between the meditator and the object meditated.

To give an example: When the yogin practices *saṃyama* on

the form (*rūpa*) of his body with a particular aim and attitude in mind, he destroys the perceptibility of the form which is the cause of perception of his body, and thus becomes invisible. The light in the eye of another person does not come into contact with the body of the yogin; the yogin has disappeared.[58]

However, the true Siddha must *overcome* the temptation of the *siddhis*, of the magical powers. Already Patañjali (*Yoga-sūtras* III. 37) warns that the possession of the *siddhis* or 'perfections' is *ultimately* an obstacle in the attaining of true *samādhi* since *all* possession implies bondage to the thing possessed.[59] It seems though, that this classical attitude was not followed by most Tamil *cittar*. There are some among them, particularly 'The Siddha with the Dancing Snake' who obviously gaze with passionate satisfaction on their own prowess, and this tone of triumph and exultation about one's own miraculous or almost miraculous abilities may be traced as recently as in some modern Tamil poets influenced by Siddha mysticism, such as in Subrahmanya Bharati.

8 *Religion and Philosophy*

From its beginnings, Yoga has been a reaction against metaphysical speculation and fossilized, empty ritualism; from its origins, it has represented a tendency towards the concrete, towards the experience of the sacred. This reaction against ritualism and scholastic speculation has always remained one of the major features of Yoga, and in its tantric and Siddha forms, this tendency has been rather stressed and revitalized.

The two most typical features of the religious conceptions of the Tamil Siddhas are anti-ritualism, the denial of current religious practices, and the denial of *bhakti*.

The Siddhas—in agreement with other tantric schools—condemn most pan-Indian religious practices, like ritual bathing and purification, worship of idols, etc., and, on a higher level, they even condemn tantric practices (like reciting the *mantras*, using the *maṇḍalas*, etc.). Such tantric practices can naturally be denied only at a particular stage in the process of realization; to other, lower levels and stages in the discipline quite a number of practices, even external practices, are still relevant in the Siddha approach.

The anti-ceremonial, anti-ritual tone of Tamil Siddha texts is universal, very strong, and the first feature to strike us when we read them.

First of all, the Siddhas or most of them, in sharp contrast to the *bhakti* tradition, refuse to allow themselves to be carried away by *idol-worship in particular temples* (a truly diagnostic feature of South Indian *bhakti*, which has been called *henolocotheism*). Cf. Civavākkiyar 126: 'Do gods become stones?' And in st. 33 he condemns ritual worship and bathing:

> 'What are temples? What are the bathing tanks?
> You fools who worship in temples and tanks!
> Temples are in the mind! Tanks are in the mind!'

In 35.1 he again says: 'You fools who perform the *pūjā*', and in many of his lines he denounces the Brahmanical way of life, repudiating the authority of the Vedas, rejecting the division between Śaivas and Śrī Vaiṣṇavas, condemning all kinds of orthodoxy and sacerdotalism.

Second, in contrast to *bhakti* which emphasizes the emotional approach, a passionate devotion to God, to one's *iṣṭadevatā* ('deity of one's choice'), the Tamil Siddha texts emphasize—apart from knowledge (see later) and Yoga practice—the character, the moral behaviour, the right conduct. In this sense, they have been called 'puritanical'. The worst sins are anger (*kōpam*), lust (*ācai*) and egoism (*akaṅkāram*). According to Akattiyar 7.1, 'if the mind is in the right disposition, it is unnecessary to say prayers'.

Third, most of the *cittar* ridicule many ritual and social customs and practices: thus for instance saliva, which is considered by the Hindus as something utterly unclean, Civavākkiyar refuses to regard as such. Cf. st. 479 where he says: 'Why should you be so fussy about saliva (*eccil*)? Why—honey is the bee's saliva; the beetle's spittle is on the flower, the cow's milk itself is mixed with the saliva of the calf.'[60] And the same poet laughs at those who bathe for cleanliness' sake and yet are impure in their hearts (stanzas 207, 209).

It is indeed difficult to extract (at least at this stage of our knowledge of the *cittar* texts) a consistent and complete theological and philosophical system from the writings of the Tamil Siddhas. However, a few essential points may be set up.

Thus, on the theological level, the Siddhas are *not* atheists, but theists and relativists. For most of them, there is a deity, *civam*, without limitation and attributes; it is the supreme thing (*parāparam*), spread everywhere (*eṅkumāy paranta*), and at the same time, within men.[61]

> 'He is not Hari, He is not the Lord Śiva.
> He is the Ultimate Cause,
> In the Beyond of Beyond,
> Transcending Blackness, Redness and Whiteness.
> Immovable.
> Try to understand:
> He is not big, He is not small.
> He is Infinite Distance,
> Immovable,
> Transcending even Supreme Quiescence.'
> (Civavākkiyar 9)

This, indeed, is great mystic poetry. On a somewhat different level, the same powerful poet says (st. 27):

> 'The slothful
> sluggards
> say: He is far, far, far
> away!
> But the Supreme It
> is spread everywhere,
> on Earth and in Heavens.
> O you poor dumb ones,
> running
> stunned and suffering
> through towns and fields and forests
> in Search!
> He is right there
> within you!
> Stand still,
> and feel Him,
> feel!'

The *world* is *real* and *not illusory* (as for example in Vedānta, or for Śrī Ramaṇa Mahāṛṣi). But it exists and endures because of man's ignorance, man's lack of knowledge. Māyā, the cosmic Illusion, endured by man so long as he is blinded by ignorance, makes possible the maintenance of the material world. Liberation (in contrast to *bhakti*, devotion) is achieved by knowledge; it is a liberation from the *idea* of evil and pain. The wretched condition of human existence and life is not due to a divine punishment, or to an original sin, or to divine test, but to ignorance—to metaphysical ignorance. That is, the ignorance consists in regarding what is ephemeral, impure, painful, and non-spiritual as being eternal, pure, blissful and spiritual. There is only one way to gain salvation: adequate knowledge (and *not* devotion, or ritual ceremonies, or simply right actions). Knowledge of what? Knowledge of the ultimate reality (*parāparam*), that is, an awakening in which the object completely identifies itself with the subject. Liberation is only becoming aware of the eternal freedom of the Spirit; it is the liberation from the idea of pain and evil. Suffering and pain cease as soon as the relation between suffering and Self ceases, that is, as soon as one understands that suffering is exterior to Spirit. Thus suffering is destroyed by ignoring it as suffering.

This kind of knowledge is obtained in *samādhi* which is achieved by practice, by psychophysiological Yoga techniques including a method of contemplation. First, of course, errors and illusions (the lowest kind of experience) as well as 'normal' psychological events must be removed and replaced by parapsychological, suprasensory and extrarational experience. For the Indian mind, the 'normal' human condition is equivalent to bondage, ignorance and suffering; freedom, knowledge and bliss are inaccessible as long as this 'normalcy' is not destroyed.

The nature of realization is such that it is completely self-contained, devoid of all discursive thought and duality of subject and object, and one is incapable to describe it. Therefore, Siddha poets must make use of images, similes and metaphors.

This knowledge (*aṟivu, ñāṉam*) is the supreme force because it solves the mystery of the universe and the enigma of the Self. It is not discursive knowledge, systematically formulated, but a knowledge gained 'by assault', through half-contemplative, half-physiological techniques.

It is like in alchemy: the 'purification' of base metals like copper and changing them into gold, results from praxis; we could never mistake the directions and the results, the achievements themselves, or rather, the knowledge of the actual processes involved in the purification of the metals. Thus, conventional, textual knowledge is not realization.

> 'O you who proclaim yourself the yogins of knowledge,
> who search after knowledge in books!
> You do not know your own hearts!
> There you should search for the light of knowledge!'
> (Civavākkiyar 453)

The teachings of the paṇḍits, even the teachings of tantric Siddhas should be transcended. Reality is attained through praxis and direct experiment. The function of the true *guru* is not to 'teach' in our sense (i.e. expounding the knowledge discursively) but to point out what is essential for praxis and direct experimentation. The preceptor's function is not discursive *teaching*, but special technical *instruction*, and *initiation*. The *guru*'s instruction stands in sharp contrast to 'bookish' (*śāstra*) knowledge. The adept is guided by the *guru* directly and experimentally; he will abandon all thoughts and their objects, and become like a child, firmly devoted to the instruction of the *guru*. 'The Vedas are not heard by one's ear. Is not true light in the utterances of the guru?[62]

All the 32 stanzas going under the name of the 'Siddha with the Earthen Ring'[63] ask basically the same question: of what avail is discursive knowledge, the *mantras*, the *mudrās*, the *tantras*, even the sacred texts like *Tēvāram*, to those who have attained realization, who possess the true knowledge (*meyñ-*

ñāni) of eightfold Yoga (*aṭṭāṅkayōkam*), to those who have conquered death,[64] having gone 'beyond the summit (*uccikku mēl*) and seen the Highest Light (*uyaroḷi*)'?[65]

On his difficult path, the yogin subjects himself to long periods of immobility in the *āsanas* or 'postures', rhythmical breathing and arrest of breath (*prāṇāyama*), immobility of thought and fixation of the mental flux, arrest and return of semen. On every level of human experience (movement of the 'gross' physical body, breathing, mental processes, sexual experience), he does the opposite of what life demands him to do. Is it a rejection of life? Is it a sort of anticipation of death?

Not in Siddha Yoga. True, certain yogico-tantric experiences are an 'anticipatory visualisation' of the processes normally set into motion by death; and some of the Siddha poets, notably Paṭṭiṉattār, found obvious pleasure in describing the process of dying and decay. But this 'anticipatory death' is an initiatory death, necessarily followed by a rebirth into the state of the *jīvanmukti*, the 'liberation in life', into the state of 'eternal present', outside of time, without personal consciousness, pure lucidity and spontaneity, a transcendental mode of being which cannot be reduced to our 'normal' categories—a rebirth after the conquest of freedom and immortality is accomplished.

A difficult and dangerous path. But worth trying.

9 *Social Attitudes*

If there is one feature which is truly common to all Tamil Siddha poets irrespective of other possible differences, it is their radical social attitude. All Tamil Siddha poets raise a protest against cast and casteism. This is an extremely important and relevant feature; however, it should not be misinterpreted. The Siddhas were not social revolutionaries, aiming at a radical structural change of the Hindu society. They disregarded, ignored, and despised the social fabric of their times, and some of them, for instance Pattirakiri, dreamt of a future age when there would be no castes: 'O when will come the time when we shall live without divisions into castes (*cātivakai*), according to the teachings of the First Kapilar?' (*Lamentations* 125.) Some of the Siddhas, notably Civavākkiyar, went further and condemned the social fabric together with those who were responsible for it, the Brahmans. In a strong stanza (38) he says that there is no distinction between a Pariah and a Brahmin woman 'in flesh, skin or bones', and that one may experiment this lack of distinction by simply sleeping with both of them. He denies the objective reality of caste: 'What *is* caste?' (45). To split up society into castes (*cātipētam*) means to conceal the true reality, since, essentially, there is only one caste: the human caste. This attitude reminds one of what an ancient Tamil poetess, Auvaiyār, expressed some centuries earlier, namely: there are only two 'castes' among men: the generous and the ungenerous.[66]

Thus, roughly speaking, the two characteristic features of the social attitude of the Siddhas are anti-casteism, and anti-Brahmanism, especially a strong stand against the Brahmans' 'pharisaic insistence on external purity and observance of rites'. One may fully agree with the following quotation: 'To denounce today caste, worship in temples and religious and agamic rituals does not require much courage, but to have done so in the centuries in which the Tamil Siddhas lived required extraordinary heroism and strength of convictions.'[67]

10 *The Poets and the Works*

'Siddhas in the Tamil land trace their origin to Agastya and various works on mysticism, worship, medicine and alchemy are in circulation as having come from his pen. Their language is too modern to be older than the fifteenth century A.D.'[68]

A few rather late yogic and philosophical poems (as well as an *Ur-grammatik* of the Tamil language) are ascribed to Agastya (Tamil Akattiyar). The poems are not much as poetry, and are not particularly impressive as to their contents either. They are rather didactic in nature, with great stress on the excellence of moral behaviour:

> 'If the mind is straight, it is unnecessary to utter *mantras*;
> if the mind is straight, it is unnecessary to raise the breaths;
> if the mind is straight, it is unnecessary to control breathing;
> if the mind is straight, prayers are straight.'
>
> (*Ñāṉam* 2)

In the *Ṛgveda*, a brief reference occurs to Agastya's miraculous birth from a pitcher (*kumbha*), but otherwise he seems to have been a historical person who composed hymns, a Vedic seer-poet, a *ṛṣi*. In the *Mahābhārata*, we already have a developed story of Agastya, including his marriage with Lopāmudrā, a princess of Vidarbha, including the motifs of Agastya's search for wealth, Agastya's drinking up the waters of the ocean, but above all of his journey to the South of India when he prevailed upon the Vindhya mountains to stop growing until he returned—which, however, he never did. In the *Rāmāyaṇa*, Agastya appears as a fighter against the demons.

But in the early Tamil works, there is no reference to Agastya the sage. It is only the rather late Old Tamil epic *Maṇimēkalai* which knows of the miraculous birth of the sage and his relation to another *ṛṣi*, Vasiṣṭha. The first reference to Agastya as the 'Father of Tamil' and the first grammarian of the language is in Nakkīrar's commentary to Iṟaiyaṉār's *Akapporuḷ* ('Grammar of Love', 8th Century A.D.). Later, medieval commentators, Nacciṉārkkiṉiyar (14th Century), and Pērāciriyar (*c.* 1300 A.D.), narrate a number of Agastya-stories, and make him the 'sage of the Potiyil mountain' (however, a reference to the sage of the mountain Poti may be found much earlier, in *Paripāṭal* xi.10–11).[69] Anyhow, this Agastya, whether he existed or not, is a very different person, a legendary and a 'cultural' hero, not the Siddha Akattiyar.[70] A grammatical treatise ascribed to him, which I had the opportunity to study (title: *Pērakattiyatiraṭṭu*, *sine dat.*), seemed to me to be rather modern, probably a late 18th–early 19th Century forgery. On the other hand, the few grammatical aphorisms contained in two medieval commentaries, seem to me to be genuine and very old. Probably this ancient Agastya has indeed composed a grammar of Tamil which has not come down to us but for the few fragments just mentioned.

The first (i.e. historically, probably the earliest) of the great Tamil Siddha poets, and in many respects the greatest one among them, is Tirumūlar.

10.1. *Tirumūlar.*

Let me begin the following short discussion of his *Tirumantiram* with a quote from M. Eliade's *Yoga* (*op. cit.* 304): 'At a certain period (probably between the seventh and the eleventh century), a new "revelation" occurred, formulated by masters who no more claimed to be original than their predecessors had done . . . , but who had reinterpreted the timeless doctrines to conform to the needs of their day. One of the essential points of this new "revelation" was that it finally completed the synthesis among the elements of Vajrayāna and Śivaist tantrism, magic, alchemy, and Haṭha Yoga.'

That 'certain period' seems indeed to have been the beginning of the development of the Siddha tradition in South India, particularly in Tamilnadu. It is usual among the Tamil Siddhas themselves to regard Tirumūlar as the greatest exponent of Yoga in South India, and as the first master of that new 'revelation' reinterpreting the timeless doctrines within the framework of the Tamil language, culture and literature. And this is how Tirumūlar very probably regarded himself. In the 'specific preface about the author' (*taṟciṟappuppāyiram*, stanzas 129 ff., esp. 156), he says: 'After I entered, by the grace of Nandi (= Śiva), the [body of] Mūlan (= Tirumūlar), by the grace of Nandi I became *catācivam* (Eternal Being); by the grace of Nandi I united with the True Knowledge; by the grace of Nandi I was.' And, more specifically, he said in st. 152:

eṉṉai naṉṟāka iṟaivaṉ paṭaittaṉaṉ
taṉṉai naṉṟākat tamiḻceyyu māṟē
'God created me well
so that I would [re]create Him [in] Tamil.'

The yogin, poet and philosopher Tirumūlar might have lived some time in the 7th Century A.D., since he is mentioned by Cuntarar in *Tiruttoṇṭattokai* ('The Anthology about the Lives of the Slave-Saints', late 7th–early 8th Century), st. 5 (7621). Umāpati Civācārya (14th Century) clearly refers to Tirumūlar as a Siddha. Tirumūlar's work *Tirumantiram* (= Sanskrit *Śrīmantra*) became part of the Śaiva canon (its tenth book).

The *Tirumantiram* is the greatest treatment of Yoga in Tamil literature, and the Śaiva Siddhānta philosophy springs from this marvellous text as from its direct source. However, for us, the chief interest of the work lies in the fact that it contains *in nuce* all or almost all the typical features of the Tamil Siddha movement.

The *Tirumantiram*, considered to represent *the* Tamil *āgama*, consists of nine sections called *tantirams* (= Sanskrit *tantra*) of different length and of very different subject-matter; the different parts of the book have not been co-ordinated into a well-knit whole, and among its more than 3000 quatrains in the *kaliviruttam* metre may be many interpolations. However, there is a fundamental unity in the work which may be defined as an attempt at the integration of the three highest roads to liberation—Upaniṣadic *knowledge*, Yogic *technique*, and *bhakti*. These three are the basic 'materia' of almost all later Siddha writings as well. In the *Tirumantiram* (1444) they are referred to as *a̱rivum aṭakkamum a̱npum*, 'knowledge, control (= Yoga) and devotion (= *bhakti*)'. Indeed, there are some moving devotional (*bhakti*-type) stanzas in the text, such as 712, 1651, 1816, 2104, 2958 (and there is much *bhakti* material in the eighth section). But much more accent is on Yoga and knowledge and in this respect Tirumūlar is the true forerunner of the Tamil Siddhas.

In st. 1463 (1490), Tirumūlar gives a very important definition of the Siddhas: the *cittar* (Siddhas) are those who 'have experienced divine light (*oḷi*) and divine power (*catti*, Sanskrit *śakti*) from within and through Yoga *samādhi*'.[71] It is indeed possible (st. 169) to experience the state of the 'world of Śiva [where] the Siddhas [live] here (*iṅkē*)', i.e. in this life, in this world—again, the main goal of tantric Yoga, and one of the chief claims of all Siddha schools.

The first section of the text (166 stanzas) deals with *a̱ram* (Sanskrit *dharma*), the cosmic and ethical order. With st. 159, Tirumūlar enters a philosophic discourse on *pati* 'Lord', *pacu* 'the Cow (i.e. Soul)' and *pācam* 'bondage', the three basic terms of Śaiva Siddhānta.[72] He enquires into the state of body and soul, he mentions the three sins of lust, anger and confusion. Knowledge (*kalvi*) is knowledge of Śiva; however, there is a distinction between Śiva, the personal God, and *civam* (grammatically and philosophically impersonal), and this second conception of the divine prevails; it is also called 'light' and 'lustre' (*cōti*, Sanskrit *joti*; or *cuṭar*), symbolized by Śiva's bull Nandi, and very often called 'the divine potter' (*kucavaṉ*).

The devotional element may be recognized in the doctrine of *aṉpu* 'affection; devotion' which *is* God. An often quoted stanza (257) says: 'Fools say: Love and god are two different things. Nobody knows that god is love. When they will realize that god is love, they will all repose in the oneness of love and god.'[73]

The second section (208 stanzas) is largely theological. It is interesting that the South of India (*teṉṉāṭu*) is conceived as *the* land of the Lord, of Śiva. This conception is present in all subsequent religious texts, chiefly in the Tamil *purāṇas*. The second section deals also with Akattiyar (Agastya), the sage who was born in a water-pot from the union of Mitra and Varuṇa with the divine damsel Urvaśī, and who became the mythical ancestor of all Siddhas. Śiva in this section is conceived as the god of the three actions of creating, preserving, and destroying the universe (e.g. 391). God Murukaṉ-Skanda, who is of a special significance to Tamil Siddhas, is mentioned in 503 ff.

For our purposes, the most important of the *tantirams* is the third one (333 stanzas) which deals with Yoga proper. The treatment contains an analysis of *yama* or 'restraints' (535–6) and *niyama* or 'disciplines' (537–9), that is, the necessary preliminaries to asceticism; of *āsanas* (Tamil *irukkai*) or 'body-postures' (540–5), *prāṇāyama* or 'rhythm of respiration' (546–58), *pratyahāra* or 'emancipation of sensory activities from the domination of external objects' (559–67), *dhāraṇā* 'concentration' (568–77), *dhyāna* (Tamil *niṉaital*) 'meditation' (578–97), and of *samādhi* (Tamil *nocippu*) 'enstasis' (598–611). We see that the *aṅgas* ('members'), the categories of physiological and spiritual practices are dealt with in the classical order as pointed out in Patañjali's *Yogasūtras* II. 29. Further, Tirumūlar deals with the results of Yoga (612 ff.), and with the eight *mahāsiddhis* or great occult powers (620–91): *aṇimā* (Tamil *nuṇmai*) 'becoming as small as an atom', *laghimā* (*meṉmai*) 'lightness', *mahimā* (*parumai*) 'illimitability', *prāpti* (*virumpiyateytal*) 'fulfilment of desires', *garimā* (*viṇtaṉmai*) 'weight', *prākāmya* (*niṟaivuṇmai*) 'irresistible will', *īśitva* (*āṭciyaṉātal*) 'supremacy over body and mind' and *vaśitva* (*kavarcci*) 'dominion over the elements'. Further, the text treats some other aspects of tantric yoga like the *khecarī* (779 ff.) 'simultaneous arresting of the mobility of breath, thought and semen', *amuritāraṇai* (825 ff.) 'arresting of urine' etc.—in short, all the principal features of tantric Haṭha Yoga are mentioned and described in this immensely important text.

Before analysing in some detail the above mentioned *aṅgas* of Yoga as described by Tirumūlar, we have to dwell upon one very important matter—namely Tirumūlar's attitude towards the human body, since this has indeed become one of the corner-stones of the Tamil Siddha doctrine.

The body, in perfect agreement with other tantric schools, acquires an importance it had never before acquired in Indian thought. It should become the instrument of man's liberation, an aid to meditation, it should be mastered and transformed into a divine body. This is a very important point, since this attitude towards one's own body as the object of perfection and the instrument of liberation is the one point according to which one can (and must) distinguish between the true Yogic Siddhas on the one hand, and 'Siddha-like' poets on the other hand.

Listen to Tirumūlar's stanza 704:

> 'Those who let the body decay, destroy the spirit;
> they will not attain the true, powerful knowledge;
> I have learned the art how to foster the body,
> I fostered the body, and I fostered the soul.'[74]

The body, for Tirumūlar, is not only a fit and suitable instrument for the soul in its career of self-discipline and search for

God (e.g. 307, 724), but the temple of God itself (1823).[75] However, he himself had to 'realize' this truth; prior to that he thought that the body was a thing with flaws and defects (*i<u>l</u>ukku*); but he has 'seen' the Ultimate Reality (*u<u>r</u>uporuḷ*) existing within the body, and he has realized that the Highest (*uttama<u>n</u>*) has made his temple (*kōyil*) in the body, and this knowledge led to his ultimate liberation.[76]

In order to transmute the body into a divine body, one must have the will to master and perfect it, and the technique of how to arrive at a perfect condition of the body as an instrument of conquering death. This technique is provided by the Haṭha Yoga.

Let us look briefly at Tirumūlar's exposition of Haṭha Yoga in the third book of his *Tirumantiram*. In 540 he says that there are eight great *āsanas* (postures) beginning with the *lotus* and ending with the *svastikāsana*.[77] In the next stanza he describes in detail the *lotus*, in 542 the *bhadrāsana*,[78] in 543 the *kukkuṭa āca<u>n</u>am* or the 'cock',[79] in 544 the 'lion'.[80]

In 545 he enumerates once more the eight chief postures, this time *bhadra*, *gomukha* or 'cowhead',[81] the lotus, the lion, *cottiram* (= *svastikāsana*), the heroic pose,[82] and the 'easy posture'.[83] All in all then, though he acknowledges (in 545) the existence of many hundreds of postures (*nū<u>r</u>u pala*), the following eight are obviously the most important for him: the lotus, *bhadra*, the cock, the lion, the cow-head, *svastika*, the heroic pose, and the easy posture. It is worthwhile noticing that all these postures are the sitting, squatting or kneeling postures, used chiefly for concentration and meditation (with the exception of 'lion' which is a typical 'arresting, immobilizing' pose). In other words: the goal is not an athletic or hygienic perfection of the body, but the mastering and conditioning of the body for other specifically Yogic purposes.

In the tenth chapter of the third book, Tirumūlar once again deals with the eightfold Yoga and its results; as many as 71 quatrains are dedicated to the eight great *siddhis*, the magical powers, which are the result of Yoga. *Bhakti* or devotion to God appears in 692 ff., while stanzas 704 ff. deal with the basic attitude towards body, and with Yogic physiology in general. The *cakras* (plexuses) are treated in 720–49, while the following quatrains deal with the 'cosmicisation' of the body. Stanzas 779–804 deal in detail with *khecarī*: arresting the breath by turning the tongue back and inserting the tip into the throat (783). Who accomplished the *khecarī*, is also able to arrest the flow of his sperm, even when he is embraced by a beautiful woman. Immortality follows (779, 787 etc.).[84] In stanzas 805 ff., sexual matters and alchemy are dealt with at some length. Thus for example in 806 it is stated that while one is sexually enjoying oneself, the breath will not go through the central conduit (*suṣumṇā*). Some of the quatrains are difficult to interpret. There is much of the mystical tantric eroticism here. This kind of Yoga is termed 'bedstead Yoga'[85]; it should be practised in the 'sixth hour', after a preliminary five-hour preparation;[86] it is practised by a man (lit. assistant, companion, friend) and a woman (lit. she-assistant, she-companion), so that she lies on him, until 'the heart overflows' but the 'spittle' (*vāy*= semen)[87] does *not* obtain.[88] The age of the woman should be twenty, and of the man thirty.[89] Stanza 814 deals with 'False Silversmiths'[90] which means those false yogins who pretend to arrest the flow of the semen but let it flow out through the 'tube',[91] and its flow is 'arrested' only in their speech.

Chapter 20 of the third book deals with the mysterious fluid in the body the cryptic name of which is 'urine',[92] and which, if drawn and lifted through yogic techniques, prevents illness and afflictions of the body; it has the function of preventive and protective substance. In 826 it is termed *civanīr* 'Śiva's fluid'. According to 827, if one drinks this *civattiṉīr* mixed with pepper (*miḷaku*), his body will change and shine like gold, and his grey hair will disappear. It seems that either urine or semen is meant, since according to 828, ignorant people discharge and waste this 'heat' (commentary, 'saltish fluid') which is contained near the 'shore' (commentary, 'under the navel'), but for those who know how to swallow it, there is eternal youth and no death. According to some Indian sources, the yogin's urine is, for example, capable of transmuting metal into gold; and there are legends about Siddha magicians who extract from urine a kind of life-elixir.[93]

The symbolic Tamil terminology concerning these matters is, in Tirumūlar's work, in full agreement with the pan-Indian tantric usage: men's semen is of the essence of Śiva and the moon; therefore the Tamil term *veḷḷi*,[94] i.e. whiteness, silver; menstrual flow and *semen muliebre* is of the essence of Śakti and of the sun; hence the Tamil term *poṉ* 'gold',[95] also *viyāḻam*, (lit. 'Thursday'). However, the cryptic, 'intentional' language, calls sperm also *vāy* 'spittle, saliva', just as for instance penis is called 'flute'.

The rest of the work is, for *our* purposes, less interesting. The fourth book has 530 stanzas and deals, roughly speaking, with *mantras* and *cakras*. The most excellent *mantra*, the 'original', the 'primeval' formula is of course *civāyaṉama*, extolled (and played with) in 903 and elsewhere. The fifth section in 154 stanzas deals mainly with *aṟam*, the moral order, the sixth section in 128 stanzas is devoted to Śaivism as the path to immortality, the 407 stanzas of the seventh book speak about the worship of Śiva in the form of the *liṅga*.[96] The eighth book (518 quatrains) deals with gnoseology, philosophy and devotion to God, and the last section in 400 stanzas is a brilliant summary of tantric mysticism.

A few additional facts should be mentioned with regard to the *Tirumantiram*. As in later Siddha works, and in contrast to classical *bhakti* (devotional literature), there is almost total absence of any local cult of the deity.[97] Though Tirumūlar is not against temple worship, the heart of the worshippers is the true seat of God (e.g. 1792), and there is almost no reference to the worship of God through ceremonies in the temples.

The use of *mantras*, of 'mystical letters' or rather 'mystical sounds' which is an indispensable part of tantric Yoga, is often stressed by Tirumūlar, and, as already pointed out, the Śaivite Tirumūlar[98] extolls above all the *mantra* of the 'five letters' (e.g. 2611, 2659, 2922). It sounds in Tamil *ci-vā-ya-na-ma*, lit. 'obeisance to Śiva', and symbolizes *ci(ṟappu)* 'excellence, greatness', *va(ṉappu)* 'grace, beauty', *yā(ppu)* 'tie, bondage', *na-(ṭappu)* 'progress', and *ma(ṟaippu)* 'screen, concealment'. A simplified form which may be uttered by anyone is just *civaciva* (2667), pronounced as *shivashiva*.

A kind of zest and zeal to go out and spread the knowledge—though it is basically a secret knowledge—may be observed in Tirumūlar (e.g. 147)[99] and this reappears in some later Siddhas.

On the social side, Tirumūlar is opposed to the caste system and seems to be rather anti-Brahmanical, if the stanzas in which he calls Brahmans gluttons and fools are not interpolated.

Though it is doubtful whether Tirumūlar was the 'greatest poet of symbolism in Tamil literature' we may more or less agree with the scholar who wrote that his poem is a 'masterpiece of mystic wisdom, robust philosophy and moving poetry'.[100]

10.2. *Civavākkiyar.*

Civavākkiyar is a simple, often crude, but almost always forceful poet. A great poet and a great mystic. The text of his stanzas, though by no means critically edited, is relatively well-established, and it may be found in all anthologies of Tamil Siddha poetry as well as in many cheap popular editions.

As far as his date is concerned, he can hardly be considered as a very early medieval poet, since his work is saturated with rather late Sanskrit loanwords.[101] He must have lived, however, before Paṭṭiṉattār the Earlier, because this canonized poet mentions him in his work *Tiruviṭai Marutūr Mummaṇikkōvai*[102]; and no other Civavākkiyar is known to the Tamil literary tradition. This fact would establish him as belonging to an age immediately preceding the 10th Century A.D. It seems that we may consider him, *after* Tirumūlar, as the greatest *early* Siddha poet, and, in many ways, as the most typical of the true Siddha poets of Tamil India. To my mind, he is a greater poet than Tirumūlar, if we evaluate purely the poetic, artistic qualities of his stanzas.

Civavākkiyar was one of the greatest rebels against the Hindu establishment, particularly against the Brahmanic order of things; he denounces the Brahmans, the authority of the Vedas and the *āgamas*, he condemns idol-worship and temple ceremonies. He is an implacable opponent of the caste system. He is against all forms of orthodoxy. He ignores the division between the Śaivites and the Vaiṣṇavites. Such rebellion against religious orthodoxy and sacerdotalism was simply ignored by the established tradition, and his poems, numbering 527 stanzas, were left out of the Śaiva canonical literature.

The use of common speech-forms, and a contemptuous tone toward sex, are the two typical qualities of his poems. 'There is a forceful clarity, shocking us sometimes by its forthright directness; he is not even afraid of using terms that prigs will call vulgar or obscene'.[103]

He is one of the major Tamil poets who have used common speech-forms in the lines of his *Song* (*Pāṭal*). In more than one way, Civavākkiyar may be considered as a landmark in the history of Tamil thought and writing.

What follows is a limited selection from the 527 stanzas of his *Pāṭal*.

I

Within the Five Realized Sounds[104]
there is the Universe and the Unlimited One
Within the Five Realized Sounds
there are the Three Primeval Ones[105]

Within the Five Realized Sounds
  there is the Beginning and the Illusion of Creation
Within the Five Realized Sounds
  there is All and Everything.

(2)

2

He is not Hari,[106] He is not the Lord Śiva.
He is the Ultimate Cause,
In the Beyond of Beyond,
Transcending Blackness, Redness, and Whiteness.[107]
Immovable.
Try to understand:
He is not big, He is not small.
He is Infinite Distance,
Immovable,
Transcending even
Supreme Quiescence.

(9)

3

The Supreme and Eternal Skill
is neither Above nor Below.
How can you build the Palace
without the Carpenter's Work?
You fools who sell your own mothers
and become enslaved!
There is no life without the Powers,[108]
none whatever!

(15)

4

You were born in the Five letters.[109] You were raised in the Five letters!
You poor people of five elements who chant the Five letters!

If you only KNEW ONE letter of the Five
and pronounced it with POWER,
the Lord in the Hall[110] would dance: Fear not! Fear not!

(20)

5

The slothful
sluggards
say: He is far, far, far
away!
But the Supreme It
is spread everywhere
on Earth and in Heavens.
O you poor dumb ones,
running
stunned and suffering
through towns and fields and forests
in Search!
He is right there
within you!
Stand still
and feel Him,
feel!

(27)

6

What are temples, tell me!
And what are sacred tanks?
O you poor slaves who worship
in temples and tanks!
Temples are in the mind.
Tanks are in the mind.
There is no Becoming,
there is no Unbecoming,
None, none whatever!

(33)

7

In bricks and in granite,
in the red-rubbed lingam,[111]
in copper and brass
is Śiva's abode—
  that's what you tell us,
  and you're wrong.
Stay where you are
and study your own selves.
Then you will BECOME
the Temple of God,
  full of His dance and spell
    and song.
(34)

8

In the Four Eternal Vedas,
In the study and reading of scripts,
In sacred ashes and in Holy Writs
And muttering of prayers
You will not find the Lord!
Melt with the Heart Inside
and proclaim the Truth.
Then you will join the Light—
Life without servitude.
(36)

9

What does it mean—a Pariah woman?
  What is it—a Brahmin woman?
Is there any difference in flesh,
  skin, or bones?

Do you feel any difference when you sleep
with a Pariah or a Brahmin woman?
(38)

10

Milk does not return to the udder once it had trickled out.
Churned butter does not enter butter-milk.
The sound of the conch does not come to life
once it had been broke.
The blown flower, the fallen fruit,
they do not jump back on the tree.
The dead
are not reborn!
Never. Never. Never.[112]
(46)

11

By the true understanding of *ōm namaśivāyamē*,
and having grasped the Truth,
by the true understanding of *ōm namaśivāyamē*,
when the Truth shines clear,
by the true understanding of *ōm namaśivāyamē*,
and having grasped the Truth,
the ŌMNAMAŚIVĀYAMĒ rests united with the Self in the
heart!
(106)

12

Like a lightning
arising
spreading
receding

and concealed,
so the Lord of my heart
  arose
    and spread
      and is concealed
within.
Like the eye
which does not know its own straight sight,
I do not know the Lord
who is within me.
As if he were
  not there!
(121)

13

Like so many forms He stands, by reason of the sound *a*,
having dressed Himself in shapes by reason of the sound *u*,
the Illusory World, by reason of the sound *ma*,
the *Civāyam* became realized by reason of the sound *ci*.[113]
(221)

14

Silence, unmoved and rising,
Silence, unmoved and sheltering,
Silence, unmoved and permament,
Silence, unmoved and brilliant,
Silence, broad and immense like the Gangā,
Silence, unmoved and increasing,
Silence, white and shining like the Moon,
Silence, the Essence of Śiva.
(332)

15

O you who proclaim yourselves the yogins of knowledge,
Who search after knowledge in books!
You do not know your own hearts!
There you should search for the light of knowledge!
(453)

16

The true *mantra* is the one which rests in the Light;
the *mantra* of Calm has taken shape and become a form,
the white *mantra* rose and ripened and became the sacred Ash,[114]
for the true *mantra* is only one: *Śivāyamē.*
(486)

17

Why, you fool,
do you utter *mantras*,
murmuring them, whispering,
going around the fixed stone
as if it were God,
putting garlands of flowers around it?[115]
Will the fixed stone speak—
as if the Lord were within?
Will the cooking vessel,
or the wooden ladle,
know the taste of curry?
(496)

18

What miserable life,
O Lord,
who dances the Dance

surrounded by dogs
in the loveless jungle
where demons gather
to feed on corpses![116]
If you truly seek
and try
to get rid of the Desire
which swells with the milk of mothers,
then look inside
and see what is hidden there,
wide:
a whirlwind of
agony
and pain
and miseries.
(500)

19

Stone, silver, copper, iron.
Out of the alloys of these base metals
different shapes were fashioned
and forms shaped
of almighty gods,
and in praising them
one will achieve
happiness.
Is that what you say?
No, no, no, no!
The Lord
is not an idol!
(522)

10.3. *Pattirakiri.*

This poet who was called the Jeremiah of Tamil literature[117] was, according to the legend, a king who was converted to

Siddhism by Paṭṭiṉattār, renounced his kingdom, and became a religious mendicant, accepting Paṭṭiṉattār as his *guru*, as his spiritual preceptor. The name is a Tamilization of the Sanskrit form Bhadragiri (or Bhartṛhari?). However, as a poet, he shows many features common with Civavākkiyar, though he is far from being so forceful, and there are only very occasional flashes of good poetry. He composed 237 distichs which go under the name *Lamentations (Craving for) True Knowledge, Meyññāṉap Pulampal.* 'The tone of the poem is one of high-pitched wailing.'[118] The short stanzas are indeed pathetic and somewhat tiresome lamentations showing utter frustration, disgust, a longing for peace, deliverance, for the sleep of death. All end with the word *ekkālam* 'when'—that is, when will come the time of my, of our, redemption? I give below seven fairly typical illustrations.

When will come
  the time
when I shall be merged with the sea of grace
and sleep sleepless sleep,[119] facing Śiva's face?
(2)

When will come
  the time
when I shall forget lustful legs and eyes,
shameful signs and faces, propagating vice?
(9)

When will come
  the time
when I get absorbed in eternal Void
with the lust for women finally destroyed?
(10)

When will come
  the time
when I rid myself from the spreading hoods
of their greedy cunts gaping like red wounds?
(11)

When will come
  the time
when I cease to think about hollow lies:
children, mother, father, sisters, other empty ties?
(13)

When will come
  the time
when I shall arrive at the bellows-mold
blowing the wind which burns actions, tricks and deceits bold?
(126)

Has the time
  now come,
when I at last know what is in the soul,
so that I may shun the fires of the shades below?
(15)

10.4. *Paṭṭiṉattār.*

There were, most probably, at least two poets bearing this name (which means 'The one who belongs to the City', that is, the City of Pukār or Kāvērippaṭṭiṉam, the Khaberis Emporion of Ptolemaios) in Tamil literary history. One, whose poems—though he is not counted among the 63 canonized Śaivite saints—were included into the eleventh book of the Śaiva canon (*Tirumuṟai*). Another, who must be regarded as the greatest poet among the Siddhas. Though there are some common features of the two, the differences are more striking, both in the content and the form of their poetry. While Paṭṭiṉattār the Siddha adopts frequently common colloquial speech forms, and his prosody is simple and forceful, often the echo of folk-songs, the earlier Paṭṭiṉattār (probably 10th Century) uses only literary Tamil, and his poetry is of high style. While, in the later poet (most probably 14th—15th Century), we have a Yogic ascetic, a man of revolt against Brahmanic and ritualistic social order, and a saint singing of the sadness in the world and accepting it with a kind of cheerful resignation, the earlier Paṭṭiṉattār, worshipping in many temples, shows definite affinity with the *bhakti* (devotional) schools of poetry. While the merit of our Paṭṭiṉattār's poems lies chiefly in their straightforward forcefulness and sincerity, the poems of the earlier poet abound in charming descriptions and captivating images. In short, the five long pieces[120] which found their way into the holy Śaivite writings, are creations of a different hand than the one which composed the haunting Siddha songs.

In most of his poems, Paṭṭiṉattār the Siddha is *the* great relativist and *the* great pessimist of Tamil literature. Life is a tragedy, an eternal interplay of contradictions, a lie, 'a tale told by an idiot'. Man is the seat of vileness and egoism, woman the great temptress. Her beauty is the most detestable thing on earth. The female body is a bag of filth. The belly compared by poets to a banyan leaf, is a shaking bag of dirt and dregs; the breasts, compared to lotus-buds, are in fact two hanging dried-up pouches parched by inner heat and scratched by the finger-nails of lusty men. The neck is full of sweat and dust and filth, and out of her hellish mouth spurts forth poison. In this respect, Paṭṭiṉattār's views agree with Patañjali (*Yogasūtras* II. 40), according to whom physical purification produces disgust with one's own body and cessation of contact with other bodies. This is a point in which 'classical' Yoga and the 'magical' Siddha Yoga significantly differ, but Paṭṭiṉattār's negative attitude towards the body is more that of a 'classical' Yogin than that of a Siddha.

While the early Tamil *cittar* are full of confidence and self-respect, Paṭṭiṉattār manifests spiritual frustration and passionate longing for peace, even in death. There is present in his poems, often, a peculiarly attractive mixture of cynicism and pathetic helplessness; of vile abuse and of moving appeal; of utter disgust and of cheerful resignation. Some of his 'beggary' stanzas have a charm of their own which has hardly been matched by any other piece of Tamil poetry.

The legend of his life says that he belonged to the *ceṭṭi* (Chetty, merchant) caste, and his real name is said to have been Vēṅkaṭa Ceṭṭi. Living in Kāvērippaṭṭiṉam, a lively harbour, he acquired great wealth by trading with Ceylon and other islands. One day, during his absence (he went to meet his ships which were reported to have returned to the port laden with golden dust), a Śaiva mendicant called at his house and left a palm-leaf wrapped in a rag with his wife. When the merchant-prince returned home, he looked into the slip of palm-leaf and found the following words: 'Not even a needle with a broken eye will follow you on your last day.' At once he gave away all his wealth, abandoned his home, and became a naked ascetic, living on alms. His sister, ashamed of his conduct tried to poison him. He then took up his abode in a forest where he begged the cowherds to bury him every day up to his shoulders, and take him out only at night fall. This rigorous asceticism cost him finally his life: the cowherds left him buried once during the night, and found him dead in the morning.

In the following selection of his poems, by no means exhaustive or even truly representative,[121] I tried to give some illustrations of the most characteristic aspects of his poetry: the opening lines of his first song, *Kōyil Tiruvakaval I*, sound like blows of a hammer, beating out the eternal and terrible truth of the unity of life and death. In *Aruḷpulampal*, the poet confesses his ignorance and helplessness. *Kōyil Tiruvakaval II* introduces his favourite theme—woman the filthy temptress, and abhorrence of one's own body. In the stanzas selected from *Tiru Ēkāmpa-mālai* we find some of the most forceful and striking lines of the poet, while *Potu* gives us rather a picture of his more mellowed, melancholic poetry, though of course in numbers 14 or 31 of this collection he has reached the peak in communicating his revulsion and disgust. The selection is closed by a long poem which reminds us at the same time of Shakespeare's famous passage II.7 in *As You Like It*, and of the *Tibetan Book of the Dead*.

1

Those who are born, die. The dead are born again.
Those that appear, disappear. Those who vanish, reappear.
Great things become small, small things become great.
Things realized become forgotten. Forgotten things, objectified.
Those who are joined, separate. Those who are parted, join again.

What has been eaten, becomes filth. What was used to adorn,
  becomes dirt.
What is enjoyed will be hated. What was hated will be enjoyed.
All these facts you have perhaps realized. And yet
All the beings, born and reborn,
You have killed. They have all killed you.

You have devoured them all. They have all devoured you.
You gave birth to all. They have all begotten you.
You have nourished them all. They have all nourished you.
You have rejoiced in wealth and suffered in poverty,
You have rested in heaven and lain in hell!

(*Kōyil Tiruvakaval I*)

2

O Lord of Madurai! O Lord of Madurai!

I do not know the origin,
I do not know the end,
I only know, o Lord,
That there's much suffering in the world.

The filth of ignorance, o Lord,
Has all the powers of my wit destroyed,
Through the results of sticking deeds
A deranged madman I became, o Lord!

By body and its actions was I stupefied,
Caught in the nets of secret rules I lied.

I roam about in jungles—Great Illusions,
sick in this world created by Confusion.

I can't forget my children and my relatives,
Attachment to the land and king does never cease.

The wish to master science does not halt,
I wish to possess Powers undissolved.

O Lord of Madurai,
O Lord!
(From *Aruḷpulampal*)

3

I am alone
Well-supplied with troubles
Disturbed by my five senses
Wandering here and there
For I have not adorned myself with the lotus of your feet
For I have not destroyed the desire the longing the lust
of women with seditious eyes
who shake the proud flesh of their shanks

I am alone
Wandering in the jungle
A basket of pus and dirt
A box of double-minded deeds
A miserable hamlet where
winds and bile and mucus dwell
A bloody mould with dirty and vile skin
A stinking vessel
Rag with four-cubit nine slits[122]

The garden of hollow devil's gourds
upon a hillock of cremation ground
A top spun by the swift rope of desire

The place of unceasing pains
A flowing vessel
The delirium of Illusion
The cage of a death-bound bird
A leather-bag for rice
A winnowing basket
A paper-kite floating in the wind
A stump cut off from the path of *dharma*[123]
A jacket sewn by the four-faced Brahma[124]

A dry leaf scorched in the flames of passion
The skin of a bulb burrowed by worms
A plump rod with forks
rising as twigs of Universal Being

A bubble on the surface of water[125]
A letter written on the wave
A few morsels for the cremation fire
am I

(*Kōyil Tiruvakaval II*)

4

Tiru Ēkāmpa-mālai

Your village does not last for ever; your family is not eternal;
even well-deserved fame goes; and women do not always last;
children and happiness are impermanent; and wealth does quickly pass;
nobody, nothing in this world is unchangeable.
Only your feet are endless Eternity,
o Ēkāmpa of Kānchi!

(13)

To bloat their flabby belly like a cotton sack
they put all the six tastes[126] into their leather-bag!

(17)

I loved this mortal vessel
stuffed with blabbering air,

this leather-bag for rice,
this torn sack wrapped in flesh,
this stinking body,
cow-stable of lust,
and roamed about and begged,
o Ēkāmpa of Kānchi,
Lord!

(27)

Why am I born on this earth,
o Ēkāmpa of Kānchi,
I who do not love your saintly feet,
I who do not speak the truth,
I who do not walk in the footsteps of the incorrupt,
I who am dull and without learning,
I who have no control over the five senses,
I who do not remain in righteousness,
I who am
evil!

(6)

When the Carpenter of Time
will fell,
like trees which are broken and bruised,
the bodies of men and women
who clasp each other in close embrace,
they will cry out
and weep,
like a stricken drum.
Will they cross the cremation ground
and reach the land
beyond?
O Lord O Ēkāmpa of Kānchi!

(2)

O Ēkāmpa of Kānchi, Lord,
arise and give me grace
not to fall into the pit
that spurts out

blood and filth!
Into the pith of women,
in their hollow trap,
women who invite
this leather-bag
which I daily stuffed
with quantities of flesh and rice,
this putrid, stinking body—
a sack for jackals,
vile and full of vice!

(34)

How many, o how many mothers were mine?
How many, o how many fathers were mine?
And then, how many women did I possess?
How many children did I beget?
How many, many births did I go through?
I do not know—
I, your foolish, foolish slave.
How many,
how many more births shall I try to waive?
O Lord, o Ēkāmpa of Kānchi,
what shall I do?

(43)

5

The jungle? The bushes? The sea-shore? The vast lands around?
The city? The hearts of towns? Comfortable houses? Hillocks and mounds?
Verandas gazing on the street? Where is the place where this lonely body can fall?
O Lord of the Great Temple of Kaḻukkuṉram!
Your feet are the help,
and life,
and all!

(*Tirukkaḻukkuṉṟam*)

6

The treasury of insolence
The granary of anger
The palace from which ignorance
will not depart
The home of falsehood
This rag of a body
full of lust and lechery
Its towering weapon
swelling into skies
  How to attain wisdom
  while worshipping you?

(*Potu* 55)

7

The fire says: It is mine.
But the worm, too, says: It's mine.
And this earth says: Well, it's mine.
But the kite says: It is mine.
And the jackal says It's mine
and wants to devour it.
And the mean dog says: It's for me!
This stinking body I cherished with love.
And what was the use?

(*ib.* 26)

8

Uttering lies so much that your tongue cracks
Hoarding riches on wealth
You lie with women who know no good
And bring forth children
So rapidly so readily
Like the poor white ants that come out when the earth cracks!

You do not know how to foster them
You will not forsake them
You have put your foot into a hole
  in the bole of a tree
Like the monkey that removed the wedge
You are caught to stay and suffer
You are caught
You!

(*ib.* 65)

9

There is no remedy to place before those men
to save them from annihilation
who
for the sake of a CUNT
perish day and night!
A cunt
wherein
day and night
flies and ants crawl
(when she had removed her saree)
wherefrom sprouts and spurts
copious pus
and bloody discharge
and slimy mucus.

(*ib.* 14)

10

Their mouth smells of flesh.
Their hairy mess is smelly.
The pus in the blackened eyes smells
and their limbs stink of their discharge.
The chasm of the vulva stinks.
Should my mind be attached

to these women
who smell of their
sensuality?

(*ib.* 31)

11

For the cool mist
there are tight rags.
There's rice in every house,
just beg and eat.
And when you are aroused,
there are fine harlots roaming in the streets.
Why then grow weary of this world?
O heart! To be so sore each day!

(*ib.* 15)

12

There is the loin-cloth for my dress
and for my pillow the outer porch.
To eat—areca-nuts and leaf.
Cool water to drink.
For precious help—
the holy names,
names of the Lord who rides the Bull.
What is there higher in this world
than the northern horn of the waning Moon?
What is there lower in this world
than the southern horn of the waning Moon?

(*ib.* 1)

13

When cold wind blows
and the Sun is gone,

there is an old abandoned dress—
just take it and cover your body.
All the world over
there's everywhere an outside porch
to lie down and sleep.
When hunger comes,
there's Śiva to give.
O heart!
There's indeed nothing that we lack!

(*ib.* 17)

14

I left the world.
I do not wish the two-fold deeds.
I do not mix with idle, useless men.
I do not listen to their speech.

I touched the state
when only Truth
remains.
I swept away
pleasures and pains.
The Highest
which is beyond the reach
of the four ancient Vedas
came
here
to me!

(*ib.* 24)

15

The eightfold Yoga
the six regions of the body
the five states

they have all left and gone
totally erased
and in the open
Void
I am left
amazed.
There is but a red rounded Moon
A fountain of white milk
for delight
The unobtainable Bliss
has engulfed me
A precipice
of light.
(*ib.* 25)

16

Utaṟkūṟṟuvaṇṇam

or

The Harmony of the Component Parts of Human Body[127]

When
an infatuated woman
and
an enamoured man
come together
and unite in affection
which yields the pleasures of sweet passion,
out of his agitation
his white semen spurts
and springs forth
and soaks her womb
mixing with her flow, (1)
and a small drop,
not bigger than a dew-drop,
enters and gyrates in her womb--
and behold,

that which was like a lotus-bud,
and like a tiny tortoise,
has eyes and body, mouth,
and ears, and legs and arms,
a human shape! (2)
It grows, the life inside,
and after ten months
the womb of the woman opens,
and a man is born.

They set his horoscope, his destiny,
an army of serfs around prepare his bed, (3)
and women dress him, caress him,
and he jumps and leaps and kicks and crawls
and falls upon the floor
and turns legs up and upside down
and sucks the nectar from the breasts
which are like a pair of young peacocks.
And day by day he grows,
and gathers knowledge, this and that. (4)
His wet lips with radiant smile
kiss happily the female servants 'round,
he sits in their laps and babbles,
saying such simple words like
'come' and 'go' and 'stay'
and utters a few names:
thus his speech is born. (5)
And then he runs about,
in lovely dress, and with a belt of gems,
eats with the grown-ups,
and in the streets plays games
with dust and clay,
and with his friends runs here and there
and so, in games and frolicking,
reaches the age of five. (6)

Then the teacher comes.
He learns the glories of his mother-tongue,

Tamil in her three shapes,
and how to write and count,
and growing up, resembles,
as so many say,
the growing crescent of the moon:
and thus he reaches sixteen years. (7)

Praised by the poets,
with fair jewels beautified,
with a well-groomed knot of hair
and wearing garlands full of humming bees, (8)
he stands in front of women,
desirous and young,
fair like the love-god,
and loses his strength—
while they, who are like peacock elegant,
devour him with their fiery eyes. (9)
He's unable to carry his desire.
He will pursue them,
he will embrace their splendid breasts,
which are like broad round pitches firm,
and he will suck the nectar off their lips,
and senselessly spend all his properties
with them. (10)

And then the remnants of his riches disappear
in suits and quarrels, actions, feuds.
And soon the pleasures go,
the youthful charm,
the fires of passion freeze. (11)

Riches are lost
and all his youth is spent,
strong teeth fall out
and eyes will lose their shine,
his hair grows grey
and wrinkled is his face,
angers and hatreds of disputes arrive.

He will now hold
an omnipresent stick
in his cold reddened hands. (12)
Bent with the weight of age
he roams about,
squatting and moving like an ape,
losing his wits,
all stiff, all deaf, and almost blind,
blabbering incongruous words. (13)
When it is time for sleep,
he coughs, his throat is dry,
and his chest is burning.

In torn rags, all numb and blunt,
mocked at by women and by boys, (14)
he wobbles 'round and his perplexity grows,
and he will fart and piss
unable to hold his urine and his stools,
and he will crawl about
in filth and dirtiness. (15)
Confused and puzzled,
staggering in speech,
his thoughts and feelings wandering about,
shaking and trembling,
he will realize
that there's no consolation in this world,
no kindness, only pain. (16)
As it is written in the Vedas four,
by the Great Teachers said:
Now the Great Calamity comes,
what will he do now,
whence will come the help?
There is now no more life on earth,
all he must do is to repay his debts. (17)

While talking, his tongue goes to sleep,
and he talks with the gestures of his hands,
soon is unable to eat

and food drips out,
and the four elements
and his breathing stop. (18)
And lo, behold,
the Messenger of Death,
like a huge mountain,
shining and black shape,
all hairy, terrible,
teeth like the crescent moon (19)—
he throws his net
and takes the life
and goes.

The others come with bowed heads,
and weep,
the wife falls in his lap and weeps, (20)
the neighbours stand around and speak:
'Well, he was very old.'
And then they, too, disperse
like cotton in the wind;
and a few stay,
propose to build a shed.
Then comes the Paraiyar
bringing his drum. (21)
They wash the corpse,
dress it and anoint,
and decorate with sandal and with wreaths.
The youngsters come and bend and take the corpse.
And they walk swiftly till they reach (22)
the burning ground.

What is this human life?
They place the body on the pyre (23)
and cover it with fuel, bathed in oil,
and then kindle the fire.
It burns and the fat melts,
and the limbs fall apart;
the bones, cracking and scorched,

sink down, deep down,
and now the body
that was man
is hardly a handful
of ash.

Be gracious to me,
who am your slave,
o Lord, to me who trusted
this body of mine! (24)

10.5. *Others.*

Iṭaikkāṭṭuc Cittar or 'The Siddha of the Pasture-Forest' belongs very probably to the later group (15th Century?) of the Tamil *cittar*. He is definitely more complicated in form and style than the earlier poets, and more literary in his diction. According to tradition he belonged to the Iṭaiyar or cowherds caste, and, indeed, the tone and imagery of his poetry suggest a pastoral milieu, probably Vaiṣṇavite-Kṛṣṇaistic.

His 'Song' is composed of 130 stanzas which differ greatly in form and content, though there is an overall unity of tone and thought; also, the whole is conceived as a dialogue between two shepherds.

From the purely literary point of view, the best of his stanzas are probably the six poems in which a honey-bee (*tumpi*) symbolizing the mind (*cittam*) is addressed (cf. stanzas 80, 81). In fact, in each group of songs, someone or other is being addressed: either one of the herdsmen, or 'the cow' (*pacu*)—these stanzas have strongly devotional, Kṛṣṇaistic (Krishna) character; or 'the base knowledge' (*pullaṟivu*), the bee, the cuckoo (*kuyil*), the swan (*aṉṉam*), the peacock (*mayil*). There is rather a strong current of devotion in all his stanzas, much 'praise', some Yoga asceticism. God is conceived as the Supreme Light (*parañcōti*, 78), as 'The Light that transcends Time and Non-Time' (st. 6), as 'boundless God' (*ellaiyil kaṭavuḷ*, 5), as the shining 'Void (*cūṉiyam*, Sanskrit *śūnya-*) of *brahma*' (2). There are some striking metaphors and similes: in particular, one should mention the part comprising stanzas 107–112, entitled 'The Milking of the Cow'. Twelve illustrations of his poetry are given below.

O praise the Light of the Lamp, the Jewel of the Skies,
the Great Light of Reflexion, the Jewel in the Eye! (47)

O praise the Light with Rays which have transgressed the Trinity of Time[128]
and hold it firm within your heart and mind! (49)

O you stony heart, why do you roam about like a fox, like a rabid dog?
Why place your wishes in this devil's ape, in this vast world? (62)

O honey-bee, fly,
knowing that we got rid of the three-fold desire![129]
O honey-bee, fly,
thinking of the *siddhis*, the Liberty's Fire!
O honey-bee, fly,
knowing that we've set up the desire of the divine!
O honey-bee, fly,
knowing that we've destroyed the worlds of design. (80)

O honey-bee, fly,
think of the Desolate Desert's fire,
O honey-bee, fly,
we've got rid of Illusion's fry.
O honey-bee, fly,
for we have reached the Fountain of Life.
O honey-bee, fly,
for you've arrived: there's Bounty, and no desire. (81)

Listen, o peacock:
there is no Freedom and no Power
for those who are
without devotion! (88)

O gentle swan,
a tree may be broken by the hurricane:

let's disperse ignorance
by the fresh wind of knowledge. (91)

O gentle swan,
a cotton bag may be destroyed by fiery flames:
sin will disappear
in the fire of ripe knowledge. (92)

O gentle swan,
salt will dissolve in water and be one with it:
be one with the Incomparable,
dissolve in *brahma*. (94)

Blow the flute in a song,
blow the flute in a song, o shepherd!
For in the Music of Silence
one attains Freedom. (98)

Milk the Cow
and don't dare to belch
Milk the Cow
to drive away approaching Death
Milk the Cow
to smother the sparks of fire
Milk the Cow
and be one with the Highest High (111)

O shepherd,
you have tied the oxen
of the three-fold body.[130]
Now there's no danger any more,
no death, no bond and bondage,
only freedom and release! (120)

Akappēy Cittar is one of the typical later Tamil Siddhas who combines deep mysticism with utmost simplicity of language and form. The name means the Siddha who invokes 'the demon of the soul'. His 90 stanzas taken together from a structured exposé of the Siddha doctrines and instructions, proceeding from the picture of the development of the universe to a total mystic 'nihilism' resulting in accepting Pure Void (*cūṉiyam*) as the only reality. In stanzas 14–15, we have exactly the same kind of speculation as that expressed by Civavākkiyar about the sounds *a*, *u*, *ma* and *ci* as symbols for the progression God→Forms→Illusion of the phenomenal world→Realization and deliverance. It is very explicit in these stanzas since Akappēy Cittar identifies *makāra* with *māyai* 'illusion' and *malam* 'filth; subtle matter inherent in the soul; sin', and *cikāram* with *mūlam* 'root, origin, source, primeval cause'. In some of the simple stanzas of this Siddha we find the most radical departure from pan-Indian orthodox philosophy and religion.

I do not exist
The Lord does not exist
The Self does not exist
The Teacher[131] does not exist (70)

Mantras do not exist
Experience does not exist
Tantras do not exist
Doctrines have been destroyed (71)

Rites are just devil's play
Knowledge—a hollow stable
The Lord is but an illusion
Everything is like that (72)

Why and whatfor to study?
Why and whatfor to act?
All set rules and all forms
have been burnt and annulled (77)

All manifested actions
you see are only Void
Those which in fact do not appear
will appear in Pure Nothingness (88)

Kutampaic Cittar or 'The Siddha with the Earthen Ring'[132] is the author of only 32 stanzas, some of them quite charming, some of them composed in symbolic language, and hence rather enigmatic. The *kutampai*, the earthen ear-ring, is for him the (female) symbol of the soul. The ultimate reality is conceived by him as *veṭṭaveḷi* 'plain, clear light'[133] or *uyarveḷi* 'the highest light'. All his stanzas are cast in a simple form with a refrain addressing the 'earthen ring' of the soul.[134]

To those who have known
that the Truth is Plain Light,
what is the use of royal grants
(o earthen ear-ring)
what is the use of royal grants? (1)

To those who have reached
beyond the Peaks for Light,
what is the use of this worldly lust
(o earthen ear-ring)
what is the use of this worldly lust? (11)

To those who have mastered
the one Tamil in three,[135]
the wise men of Truth
(o earthen ear-ring)
what is the use of selective rules? (10)

Stanzas 27 and 28 have several layers of meaning; the plain, apparent meaning deals with such inelegant and coarse matters like vegetables, spices, and fruit-juices; but of course these are symbols derived from the Siddha medicinal system. Pepper (*miḷaku*) and dry ginger (*cukku*) belong to the traditionally established curative combinations of the 'three remedies' (called *tirikaṭukam*)[136] or 'six remedies' (*ēlāti*)[137] widely used in Siddha medical practice. Already some of the early Tamil literary works have been named after herbal medicines:[138] the books were supposed to contain words of advice and solace which were capable of healing the afflictions of the mind and heart just as the herbal remedies heal the afflictions of the body.

When there is onion,
pepper and dry ginger,
what is the use of other remedies
(o earthen ear-ring)
what is the use of other remedies? (27)

To those who have climbed
on top of the Hill and drunk
the juice of fresh mango fruits
(o earthen ear-ring)
what is the use of coconut milk? (28)

Stanza 28 is quite well-known among the Tamils and is always interpreted metaphorically. According to one of my Siddha informants (the one who had the medical practice in Mylapore, Madras, and was inclined to derive from the texts rather a medical than a metaphysical information), the mixture of dry pepper and dry ginger boiled with an onion-brew was an effective remedy against headaches caused by cold. But for other Siddhas, the onion, the pepper, and the dry ginger are symbols of other things either on the tantric or on the purely spiritual planes. The onion for instance lends itself to symbolic interpretation because of the possibility to peel off its successive skins one by one[139] like one peels off the unrealities, illusions and falsehoods of the material world; also, because of its smell which is so penetrating and perseverant,[140] brings tears into the eyes, and so on. There is, to be sure, not much poetry in the stanzas of this Siddha.

Probably the most popular among all Tamil Siddha poets, and perhaps the most outspoken and crude one is *Pāmpāṭṭic Cittar* or 'The Siddha with the Dancing Snake' whose poems will close our selection. I am convinced that there is no

Tamilian who would not know his song which begins with the words *nātarmuṭi mēlirukkum nākap pāmpē* (20) 'O cobra, you who live on the crown of the Lord's head'.[141] His work, consisting of 129 stanzas, is definitely structured, showing a progress from the praise of the Lord Śiva, through the rejection of wealth, women, and body, to the vision of the deity, teachings of the spiritual leader, and final instruction how to attain Siddhahood and liberation. The first nine stanzas are dedicated to the praise of God (cf. st. 9), the next ten are in praise of the preceptor (*guru*) (cf. st. 16;) the next five stanzas are about the Dancing Snake; fifteen stanzas follow which describe the prowess of the Siddhas (cf. st. 27, 28, 30, 31, 32); the next ten stanzas speak about the renunciation of wealth; the ten stanzas which follow reject women (cf. 51, 52, 59); ten stanzas are dedicated to the ephemeral nature of human body (cf. st. 63, 64), and the next decade to the cessation of all ties (cf. 70, 76, 78); the next twenty stanzas are on the vision of the deity and the teachings of the *guru*; twelve stanzas deal with the vision of Truth (cf. 110); then, in a different rhythm (beginning with st. 112), we have eighteen stanzas containing the concrete instruction how to obtain liberation, and describing again the qualities and the powers of the Siddhas (cf. stanzas 115, 123, 125). It is especially this last portion which is very valuable since it is rather concrete and detailed.[142] This truly powerful 'poet of the powers' must have lived sometime in the 14th–15th Centuries, not earlier; the most probable date would be 1400–1450, based on the chronological assessment of the poet's lexical use.[143]

There has hardly been, even in the Siddha tradition, a poet asserting the incredible powers of the *cittar* in a more vigorous manner and a more straightforward language. Also, in his stanzas about women and the body, he has used, like Paṭṭiṉattār, and perhaps even more so, rather vulgar, even obscene language, and in this respect, too, he will hardly find a match in Tamil poetry. Many of his stanzas, though, expound Siddha doctrines in the typically symbolic language: thus it is Pāmpāṭṭic Cittar who discusses the awakening of the Kuṇḍalinī Śakti which lies coiled like a snake, and her progress through the *cakras*.

He is also supposed to be the author of a toxicological treatise, the *Cittarārūṭam*.[144]

1

Dance o snake
for you've seen
the Deluge of Bliss
which stands Outside and Apart
like the Beginning and the Source of all life and all worlds
after it had given life to all life and all worlds
in its Divine Play (9)

2

Who's able to describe the powers of the *guru*
For he knows how to pass his soul
from one body to another at his will
Dance o snake
and worship always the true *guru*
who shows us how to attain
above all
Freedom (16)

3

We can make a pillar appear
like a tiny straw
and a straw we shall transfigure
into a huge mount.

We can change men into women
and pricks
into cunts.

Like a ball lift Eight Big Mountains[145]
throwing them about.
All the Seven Oceans[146] drink and spit them out.
Enter burning fire
and waters.
And a tiger fight!

We can change the burning sunshine
into cooling Moon.
We can transform all the Three Worlds[147]
into shining gold.
We can even ruin and ravage
all this immense world!

We shall flatten
      overpower
            subjugate
the King!
We shall make new, other creatures
like those, made by God.
We shall live on equal footing
with the Lord of Lords! (27, 28, 30, 31, 32)

4

We have swallowed the milk of the Siddhas
and hence
we say fie
and we are disgusted with women
who have eyes like beetles
and breasts like balls
We have killed and eaten the hawk of Death
the god who rides the black buffalo (51)

5

They would compare the dry skin
of the round breasts
to the golden Mount Mēru[148]
Those who fell into the well
of the foul-smelling cunt
will perish
Be sure of that o dancing snake (52)

6

The saffron paste on a pitcher of dirt
Coloured skin over a swarming crowd of worms
Stinking slime in the wet hole
We have pushed it all away
Dance o snake (59)

7

Pus and filth and thick red blood and fat
All together making up an ugly smelling pitcher
Now if that breaks
Dog and jackal and large goblins and hawks
will cry: It belongs to us
And they will gobble it (63)

8

Like a bubble that arises on the surface of water
and perishes
so indeed perishes this unstable body
Therefore

adhere to the Creator of so many lives in so many worlds
Begin by loving Him
and dance o snake (64)

9

Like the drops of water that will not adhere to the leaf
  of the lotus
such is the desire of the world
Push it away leave it and
worship and adore adore o dancing snake
the feet of the dazzling
blazing brilliant white light
shining everywhere (70)

10

Look, we have killed,
with the sharp goad of reason and arguments
the insane fury of the mad elephant
called Anger.
We have formed friendship with the Light:
with the Thing that is Pure Intelligence (67)

11

Use as your riding beast
the horse of reason
Use as your bridle
knowledge and prudence
Mount firmly your saddle of anger
and ride in bright serenity
o dancing snake (78)

12

Listen eagerly:
For I shall reveal to you the great cure
how to sever the chain of births and deaths.
Open the door of thought
which shuts the undefended mind,
and know the MEANS,
o dancing snake! (110)

13

One must delve deep
into the Self of the Heart
and a gentle Fire start
and know what means In and Out
and flowing through the Net of Streams
beyond false perceptions and dreams
stand firm and gaze above the nose and eyes[149]

Seeking the Self the Glowing Supreme Light
I saw o snake the Feet of Bliss and Might (115)

14

We shall kindle the fire in the rift among castes
We shall plant our staff in open market places
We shall play and dance on the crossroads and in the streets
We shall establish friendships in undesirable houses
We shall hang about poking and prying and loitering
We shall enjoy fornicating lusty women
Because
All the five Primeval Brahmas are fools
This is what you do and say o dancing snake[150] (123)

15

We shall lock the snake in the vessel of the eye of a needle
We shall wander about around the entire world
We shall forget the stained defiled births
We shall shake with Dance in the Outside and Apart
We shall give away like prey our filthy senses
We shall climb the top of our Minds and dance
We shall devour all speech and all writs
We shall become Free from Birth and Death (125)

11 *Conclusions. Siddha Doctrines in Modern Indian Thought*

The doctrines of the Siddha, in their blend of Yoga and magic tantrism, represent a very archaic modality of spirituality which has survived nowhere else, and which has remained in existence down to our day, as a kind of 'living fossils', strangely modern. It is important that the yogins and the Siddhas contributed to the spiritual unity of India, by their frequent, in fact constant journeys throughout the country, and by their monasteries. During certain periods, Siddha doctrines penetrated the whole of India. Since, however, they represent the reaction against ritualism and metaphysical speculation, and since the language of the Siddhas is often offensive, vulgar and obscene, there has always been resistance to various schools of Siddhism on the part of the 'establishment' and orthodox Hindu circles.

As already mentioned and stressed above, in the southernmost part of India, in the state of Tamilnadu (Madras), Siddha doctrines have survived probably better than anywhere else in India and are still a very vital undercurrent which has played an important role in modern and contemporary poetry and prose, religious thought, social fabric, and in medicine and science. However, one must never forget the basically esoteric 'secret' nature of the doctrines. The phenomenon has not been studied properly in any of its manifestations. Far from it. In fact, it has hardly ever been scratched on its surface, and the present book is a far cry from any systematic and detailed treatment of Siddhism in the Tamil land. However, it will probably for the first time draw the attention of those who may and should be interested—of Oriental scholars, or religionists, of medical scientists, and of young people who will find, I am almost certain of it, more than one common feature with these poets of disgust and protest.

In modern Tamil literature, the Siddha poetry has left some deep traces. An important early modern poet, Svāmi Rāmaliṅka Piḷḷai (1823–1874), the author of the *Song of Divine Grace*, has been so much influenced by Siddha thought that some of his poems have been actually included into the several recent editions of Siddha poetry. The great national poet of Tamilnadu, Subrahmanya Bharati (1882–1921) has called himself a Siddha; and, indeed, not only the form and language of some of his songs, but to a great extent the imagery and the content is derived directly from Siddha poetry. One could point even to some contemporary authors and discover doubtless influence of some of the more popular Siddha poets.

The most authentic modern Indian 'saint' and religious thinker, Bhagavān Śrī Ramaṇa Mahārṣi (1879–1950), though far from being a Siddha himself, knew intimately Siddha doctrines, and quite often spoke about them, even if mostly very critically.

'There is a certain school of thinkers who would not call anyone a *jnani* whose body is left behind at death. It is impossible to conceive of a *jnani* attaching such importance to the body. But there is such a school—the Siddha School.'[151] Further: 'Some have maintained that the body can be made immortal and they give recipes, medical and other, for perfecting this body and making it defy death. The Siddha School (as it is known in the South) has believed in such a doctrine . . . But all people, after writing long treatises on the indestructibility of their body, after giving medical recipes and yogic practices to perfect the body and keep it alive for ever, pass away one day!'[152] Elsewhere, Śrī Ramaṇa does not argue against the Siddha teachings, he just mentions them or even uses them, for example in *Talks* (1968) 421–2 where he tells the story of Kaṭuveḷi Cittar. In the same work (551) this amazing and saintly man says: 'Self-realization may be accompanied by occult powers or it may not be. If the person had sought such powers before Realization, he may get the powers after Realization. There are others who had not sought such powers and had attempted only Self-realization. They do not manifest such powers. These powers may also be sought and gained even after Self-realization. But then they are used for a definite purpose, that is, the benefit of others.' For Śrī Ramaṇa, the 'highest perfection (*siddhi*)' is 'that which results in peace'. Though he has never embraced Siddha teachings, the Maharshi's use of some Siddha thought and terminology (cf. ftn. 119), and his testimony concerning the occult powers which he has obviously regarded as very real, is no doubt very interesting and quite important.

For the contemporary Western man, it is probably the medical component of Siddhism, and the scientific aspects of the doctrines in question, which are most engaging and interesting (apart from enjoying some Siddha poems simply as poetry of a particular sort). Such facts as the discovery of seminal animalcules ascribed to Agastya, and his supposed performing the trephination of the skull were mentioned above. One Siddha (Kōrakkar) is said to have introduced the use of *Cannabis indica* into the Siddha medical practice, and hence the weed, and hashish, is known as *Kōrakkar mūli* or Kōrakkar's drug.[153]

Most interesting are, of course, those detailed medical and chemical treatises which contain concrete diagnostic, therapeutic, pharmacological and toxicological data and instructions. These, however, are the least known of all Siddha texts. Western medicine just about begins to realize their importance.[154] In India itself, it is only very recently that the government of Tamilnadu (Madras) is willing to encourage research into Siddha medicine. But there are definite signs of a revival.

I would like to mention here a few facts which might draw the attention of Western medical science to some remarkable points in the Siddha teachings.

One of the most interesting medically oriented Siddha authors is Tēraiyar, according to tradition Agastya's pupil and a prolific writer on the subjects connected with his profession of a most skilful healer. All his works have perished except a treatise on medicine entitled *Cikāmaṇiḍveṇpā*, a treatise on pulsation (*Nāṭikkottu*) and the fragments of a treatise on hygiene (*Nōyaṇukāviti*).[155]

Let me quote just two stanzas from Tēraiyar's fragmentary treatise on hygiene.

> We will eat only twice, not three times a day;
> we will sleep only at night, not during the day;
> we will have sexual intercourse only once in a month;
> we will drink water only at meals, though we may feel
> thirsty;
> we will not eat the bulbous root of any plant except that of
> *karaṇai*;[156]
> we will not eat any unripe fruit except the tender plaintain;
> we shall take a short walk after a friendly meal;
> what has Death then to do with us?
>
> Once in six months we shall take an emetic;
> we shall take a purgative once in four months;
> once in a month and a half, we shall take a *naciyam*;[157]
> we shall have the head shaved twice in a fortnight;
> once every fourth day we shall anoint outselves with oil and
> bathe;
> we shall apply collyrium[158] to the eyes every third day;
> we shall never smell perfumes or flowers in the middle of
> the night;
> what has Death then to do with us?

Elsewhere, Tēraiyar speaks of the necessity to drink only boiled water at meals, to dilute one's yoghurt with water, to use only melted butter, to give free way to alvine discharges, and to behave cautiously vis-à-vis sexual pleasures.

Tēraiyar lived probably in the 15th Century.

But even an early author like the celebrated Tirumūlar has composed stanzas which may be of interest to Western medicine. Interesting is, for instance, his definition of medicine which sounds very modern in its insistence on prevention, and in its view that both body and mind should be given equal attention:

> Medicine means the prevention of physical illness;
> medicine means the prevention of mental illness;
> prevention means to avert illness;
> medicine therefore is the prevention of death.

Another stanza which is ascribed to Tirumūlar deals with the diagnostic methodology:

> By the examination of the pulse, by voice, by touch—
> as the ancients said—
> by elongated eyes and the indications on the tongue,
> by the tired body, by stools and urine
> they will easily know the affecting disease.

Another interesting point is the preoccupation of the Siddhas with the transformation of matter and the insistence of some presumably modern-oriented Siddhas that they work with anti-matter (*etirpporuḷ*). The theory that atomic particles have mirror images opposite to them in electric charge and magnetic field was I think first proposed by the English scientist and Nobel prize winner P. A. M. Dirac in 1927. In 1955, some anti-particles of matter were discovered at the University of California in Berkeley (O. Chamberlain, E. Segre), and in 1965, L. M. Lederman produced the anti-nucleus. Finally, in 1971, the Soviet physicists have produced anti-helium 3. All these accomplishments may contribute to the long-discussed theory that there may be an entire universe of anti-matter—a kind of anti-universe—or at least isolated deposits of anti-particles in our universe.

In the light of these accomplishments of contemporary Western scientists it sounds indeed quite astonishing to hear the Siddhas mention anti-matter when discussing their miraculous (or, should we rather write, 'miraculous'?) powers. When one of my own Siddha informants accomplished to produce, out of apparent nothing, a very substantial chunk of matter, he —rather reluctantly—explained his feat as a kind of game with anti-matter.

According to L. Kameswaran,[159] Howard Bentley declared in 1958 to J. Thorwald, the author of *Science and Secrets of Early Medicine*,[160] that a time will come when the history of Indian medicine will have to be rewritten. There can be hardly any doubt about that now. What is needed first is a massive, detailed, and critical study of all Siddha texts available.

Appendix

Hints regarding the physical and mental health
(by one of my Siddha informants: Madras, 1968)

Food

1. Eat only if hungry.
2. Never eat when tired; never eat when emotionally upset.
3. Chew your food thoroughly, well mixed with saliva.
4. Between meals, eat only fresh fruit, or fresh fruit juices.
5. Add to your daily diet great quantities of *mōr*, i.e. yoghurt or buttermilk.
6. Always eat fresh fruits and raw vegetables, if possible.

Sleep

7. Try to sleep at least eight hours daily. The best sleep is before midnight. Sleep with your window open, naked, head toward the North, the feet slightly raised.

Sun

8. Take frequent sun-baths; however, do not get too much sun at one stretch.

Breathing

9. Breathe deeply, rhythmically, slowly, regularly and relaxedly. Be conscious of the speed and rhythm of your breath.

Walking

10. Walk at least two hours daily.

Sex

11. Regular and frequent sexual intercourse is beneficial. However, be master, not slave of your sex-life. Oral-genital sex is not harmful; on the contrary, it is often desirable. Visualize yourself as the creative Śiva, and your partner as your (i.e. Śiva's) *śakti*, energy. Let her lie on you, and drink your sperm; let you suck her discharge of pleasure (*curatanīr*).

Mental attitudes

12. Never give up. Never be idle. Try to maintain always a cheerful and positive attitude. There is no harm in satisfying a desire, when the satisfaction destroys it. Do not suppress forcibly any desire. Liberation is always here and now with you. If you cannot believe in god, it does not matter. Believe in yourself, in your own existence. Find out the source from which you came.

Bibliography

LIST OF BOOKS CITED IN THE TEXT (other than Sanskrit and Tamil)

Bernier, François, *Voyages de François Bernier, docteur en médecine de la faculté de Montpellier*, Amsterdam, 1723.

Briggs, George W., *Goraknāth and the Kānphaṭā Yogīs*, Calcutta, 1938.

Brosse, T., *Etudes expérimentales des techniques du Yoga*, Paris, 1963.

Chitty, Simon, Casie, *The Tamil Plutarch*, Colombo, 1946.

Compte rendu du 1er Congrès International des Sciences neurologiques de Bruxelles, **3**, Pergamon Press, 1959.

Conditionnement et réactivité en électroencephalographie, Paris, Masson, 1957.

Dasgupta, Shashibhusan, *Obscure Religious Cults as Background of Bengali Literature*, Calcutta, 1946.

Devaraja Mudaliar, A., *Day by Day with Bhagavan*, Tiruvannamalai, 1968.

Eliade, Mircea, *Yoga, Immortality and Freedom*, Princeton, 1969.

Filliozat, J., *Magie et médecine*, Paris, 1943.

——, *La doctrine classique de la médecine indienne*, Paris, 1949.

Hittleman, R., *Yoga*, Englewood Cliffs, 1964.

Indian Historical Quarterly, **IV**, 2, 1928.

Indian Journal of Medical Research, **49**, 1, January 1961.

Jesudasan, C. and H., *A History of Tamil Literature*, Calcutta, 1961.

Limites de l'humain, Paris, Etudes carmélitaines, 1943.

Meenakshisundaran, T. P., *A History of Tamil Literature*, Annamalainagar, 1965.

Montaigne, Michel de, *Essays*, Penguin Books, 1967.

Mookerjee, R. K., *Rasa-jala-nidhi; or, Ocean of Indian Chemistry and Alchemy*, Calcutta, 1926–38.

Nau, H., *Prolegomena zu Pattanattu Pillaiyars Padal*, Halle, 1919.

Pandey, R. B., *Indian Paleography*, Banaras, 1952.

Proceedings of the Second International Conference-Seminar of Tamil Studies, I, Madras, 1971.

Ray, Prafulla Ch., *A History of Hindu Chemistry*, Calcutta, 1904–9.

Renou, L. and Filliozat, J., *L'Inde classique, manuel des études indiennes*, Paris, 1947–53.

Schulz, J. H., *Das autogene Training (Konzentrative Selbstentspannung)*, Stuttgart, 1960.

Stearn, J., *Yoga, Youth and Reincarnation*, New York, 1968.

Subramania Aiyar, A. V., *The Poetry and the Philosophy of the Tamil Siddhars*, Tirunelveli, 1957.

Talks with Sri Ramana Maharshi, Tiruvannamalai, 1968.

Taylor, W., *Oriental Historical Manuscripts, in the Tamil Language*, Madras, 1935.

Theos, Bernard, *Hatha-Yoga, The Report of a Personal Experience*, New York, 1944.

Thorwald, J., *Science and Secrets of Early Medicine*, London, 1963.

Tolkien, J. R. R., *The Tolkien Reader*, New York, 1966.

Wiener Zeitschrift für Nervenheilkunde und deren Grenzgebiete, Wien, Springer, 1958.

Also, *International Herald Tribune*, 20.2.1971, *The Listener*, 30.5.1968, *Press médicale*, Paris, 14.10.1936.

The best authentic book on Yoga to be recommended to Western readers is Swami Vishnudevananda, *The Complete Illustrated Book of Yoga*, introd. by Dr. Marcus Bach, Pocket Books, New York, 1972.

NOTES TO THE FOREWORD

1. Tamil is a Dravidian language of South India, spoken by 30,465,442 inhabitants of the State of Madras (Tamilnadu), by about 2,500,000 in Ceylon, further by Tamil settlers in Burma, Malaysia, Indonesia and Vietnam (about 1 mil.), East and South Africa (260,000) and elsewhere in the world where the Tamils, 'the Greeks of India', settled as merchants, intellectuals, moneylenders, bankers, and plantation-workers. The earliest literary monuments of the language belong to ca. the 3rd Century B.C.

2. A. V. Subramania Aiyar, *The Poetry and the Philosophy of the Tamil Siddhars*, An Essay in Criticism, S. Mahadevan, Tirunelveli, 1957.

3. Let me at the very beginning briefly state my present *personal* attitude towards the Tamil Siddha school of thought. I am a person of strong empirical leanings and with a hearty taste for concrete verifiable data. It is precisely *because* I had the opportunity of empirically verifying some of the facts which the *cittar* claim as their specific abilities and fruits of their discipline and knowledge, that I am inclined to take some of these matters very seriously. Thus I was able to find out how very successful their treatment of some disorders and diseases can be (on my own person, and on others); I was also able to witness some of the *siddhis*, the special 'occult' powers, and since more people were present at the occasions, some of them scientists holding unshakable materialistic views, and yet they were convinced, I have hardly been a victim of delusion of any kind. I am convinced that the Siddhas possess some extraordinary abilities, and an exceptional knowledge concerning 'body' and 'mind', and that these abilities and this knowledge should be studied carefully and with awesome attention precisely at this point in the development of modern science when, to quote N. Chomsky, the American linguist (*The Listener*, 30 May 1968) 'the concept of "physical" has been extended step by step to cover anything we understand', so that 'when we ultimately begin to understand the properties of mind, we shall simply . . . extend the notion "physical" to cover these properties as well.'

The fact that the Tamil Siddha thinkers seem attractive and worth a great deal of attention does not at all mean that I subscribe to the notion that we in the West should simply accept one of the solutions of the eternal problem of our 'temporality and historicity'—the solution proposed by Indian thinkers. Even less would I accept that kind of philosophical syncretism which was initiated by the Theosophical Society and continued since then, mostly in the United States, and which I detest and, in agreement with Eliade, would rather call 'spiritual hybridism'. In fact, one of the reasons for writing this book is precisely the conviction that we should know and try to understand a thought which is an integral and important part of Indian spirituality in its 'pure' and 'unadulterated' form, since it has been preserved as a largely esoteric teaching in texts which are difficult to obtain and composed in a language difficult to understand.

NOTES TO CHAPTER 1

4. Mahāvidvān M. V. Venugopala Pillai was born on 31 August 1896 at Mettupalayam near Saidapet, Madras. He belonged to a family so poor that he was unable to study regularly. Working hard during the day for his livelihood, he studied in free evening-schools, maintained by a group of philanthropists in Madras. Later he specialized in Tamil language and literature, and in 1920 he became himself a Tamil teacher at the Muthialpet High School in Madras. At the same time, he joined the Fabricius High School as the Senior Tamil Pandit, where he served for 18 years. In 1938 he retired because of ill-health and has since devoted his attention fully to writing and editing classical works. In 1967, he was awarded the title *Centamiḻk kaḷañciyam*, 'Encyclopaedia of Classical Tamil'. His knowledge is indeed encyclopaedic. He is one of the last great traditional pandits who combine vast knowledge, stored in their amazing memory, with meticulously exact traditional methods.

5. Hence it was unnecessary—even unwanted—to write the texts down, though examples can be found of teachers using written texts to support their bad memory. But this was regarded as a bad habit, cf. Patañjali's *Mahābhāṣya* as quoted by R. B. Pandey, *Indian Palaeography*, Banaras, 1952, p. 15, footnote 2.

6. With the generous help of Mrs Albertine Gaur of the Library of the British Museum.

7. The pre-Aryan, Dravidian god of youth and beauty, of virility and victorious war, Murukaṉ, was identified with Kumāra, 'the Adolescent', Skanda, 'the Spurt of Semen', Subrahmaṇya, 'Dear to the Brāhmaṇās', the

lord of the armies, the great captain, one of the two sons of Śiva. Ultimately, several ancient South Indian divinities—apart from Murukaṉ—collapsed into this one particular deity (chief among them Vēlaṉ, 'the Spear-bearer' and Ceyyōṉ, 'the Red One') who is rather important in Yoga as the power of chastity, the power of the virile seed, preserved through penance; so long as complete control is not attained in the practice of Yoga, Kumāra 'is not born'; only by making (the sublime) semen rise through the central channel of the sublime body up to the 'mouth of fire' in the sixth centre where it is consumed, the yogin becomes complete master, and 'Skanda is born'.

In South Indian iconography, Murukaṉ is usually shown as a handsome youth with one or six heads, two or twelve arms, dressed in red, holding a bow and arrows, a sword, a thunderbolt and an axe, but above all his spear (*vēl*) which never misses its mark; he rides on the peacock, the killer of serpents, (serpent=cycle of years; peacock=killer of Time, and Death; important image in tantric Yoga!). His emblem is the rooster. His banner is red as fire. He has two wives, Teyvayāṉai and Vaḷḷi, the beautiful daughter of the hunters. The motif of erotic plays with Vaḷḷi is a typically pre-Aryan Tamil motif; a local mythus of Murukaṉ, current in Northern Tamilnadu, and incorporated into the Skanda cycle in the Tamil version of the *Skanda-purāṇa*, Kacciyappa's *Kantapurāṇam* (1625 A.D.), a lovely epic of 15,345 lines.

NOTES TO CHAPTER TWO

8. Michel de Montaigne, *Essays*, I, 19.

9. It is sufficient to throw a casual glance at the front page of any big Western newspaper to see this attitude reflected in concrete actions: thus for example the front page of the *International Herald Tribune* of 20 February 1971. There is a report on West European governments having approved the construction of a giant atom smasher capable of 310 million electron volts; by the time it is ready, the U.S. will have an accelerator capable of 500 million electron volts; but Europe's accelerator will ultimately be boosted up to 800 million electron volts (and so on?). On the same page, there is another report on the discovery of a jaw-bone of an Australopithecus Africanus, adding millions of years to man's past, and filling the evolutional gap between our direct ancestor and the 'man-ape' who lived about 14 million years ago.

10. Cf. J. R. R. Tolkien, 'On fairy-stories', *The Tolkien Reader*, Ballantine, New York, 1966.

11. The list of the 18 *cittar* who possess the 'eight powers': Akattiyar, Pōkar, Kailāyanātar, Kōrakkar, Tirumūlar, Caṭṭaimuṉi, Koṅkaṇar, Kūṉkaṇṇar, Iṭaikkāṭar, Nantīsvarar, Puṇṇākīcar, Urōmariṣi, Maccamuṉi, Kūrmamuṉi, Camalmuṉi, Vācamuṉi, Piramamuṉi, Cuntarāṉantar (accord. to *Cittar periya ñāṉakkōvai*, ed. by Aru. Rāmanātaṉ, 3rd ed. 1968). Another list was provided by my Siddha informant: Nanti, Akattiyar, Mūlar, Puṇṇākīcar, Naṟṟavattup Pulattiyar, Pūṉaikkaṇṇar, Nantiṭaikkāṭar, Pōkar, Pulikkaiyīcar, Karuvūrār, Koṅkaṇavar, Kālāñci, Cinti Eḻukaṇṇar, Akappēyar, Pāmpāṭṭi, Tēraiyar, Kutampaiyar, Caṭṭaināṭar.

There exists an alphabetical list of 25 Tamil Siddhas with their caste-origin given, and the place where they lived or, as some believe, where they still 'dwell', eternally, since they are immortal. I have reserved the list for this footnote since not every reader is necessarily interested in such details.

Name	*Caste*	*Place of abode*
Akattiyar (Agastya)	*vēḷāḷar* 'agriculturalist'	Aṉantacayaṉam
Akappēy	*vēḷāḷar* 'agriculturalist'	Aḻakarmalai
Aḻukaṇṇar	*Cīṉattu ācāri* 'A Chinese preceptor'	Aḻakarmalai
Iṭaikkāṭar	*iṭaiyar* 'shepherd'	Tiruvaṇṇāmalai
Kamalamuṉi	*uvaccar* 'temple-drummer'	Tiruvārūr
Karuvūrār	*kaṇṇāḷar* 'artificer'	Karuvūr
Kāḻāṅkinātar	*Cīṉattu ācāri* 'a Chinese preceptor'	Kāñcīpuram
Kutampai	*iṭaiyar* 'shepherd'	Māyūram
Koṅkaṇar	*kaṉṉaṭa iṭaiyar* 'Kannaḍa shepherd'	Tiruppati
Kōrakkar	*kaḷḷar* 'robber'	Pērūr (Kōvai)
Caṭṭanātar	*ciṅkaḷavar* 'Singhalese'	Tiruvaraṅkam
Cuntaranāṉantar	*vēḷāḷar* 'agriculturalist'	Maturai
Taṉvantiri	*kurukkaḷ* 'Brahmin priest'	Vaittīsvarar kōyil
Tirumūlar	*vēḷāḷar* 'agriculturalist'	Tillai (Citamparam)
Tēraiyar	*pirāmaṇar* 'Brahmin'	Potikaimalai
Nanti	*pirāmaṇar* 'Brahmin'	Kāci (Benares)
Patañcaliyar	*kaḷḷar* 'robber'	Rāmēsvaram
Pāmpāṭṭi	*kōsāyi* 'a North Indian'	Viruttācalam
Puṇṇākīcar	*kaṉṉaṭa iṭaiyar* 'Kannaḍa shepherd'	Nāṅkuṉēri
Pulastiyar	*ciṅkaḷavar* 'Singhalese'	Yāḻppāṇam

Pūṉaikkaṇṇar	*ekiptiyar* 'Egyptian'	Ekiptu (Egypt)
Pōkar	*ciṉatēcakkuyavar* 'Chinese potter'	Paḻaṉi
Maccamuṉi	*cempaṭavar* 'fisherman'	Tirupparaṅkuṉṟam
Vāmatēvar	*ōtuvār* 'Vedic teacher'	Aḻakarmalai
Vāṉmīkar	*vēṭar* 'hunter'	Eṭṭikkuṭi

The ones whose names are printed in italics were dealt with in some detail. This list (as well as the other lists) is indeed very interesting; it is obvious that some historical information got mixed with a lot of fiction, and obviously one should take these lists of the *cittar* very carefully indeed. A detailed discussion of these lists cannot be at all entered into in a book like this; however, one should notice, (a) a relatively small number of Brahmins (b) the 'international' cast: apart from Tamils and probably North Indians, there are Kannaḍa Siddhas, Singhalese and even Chinese, not to speak of the Egyptian! (c) it is obvious that most of the names are strange nick-names (like 'The One with the Eyes of a Cat') or names derived from the texts of their songs (like 'The Siddha with the Dancing Snake'). Taking all this information extremely carefully, we may still arrive at one valid general conclusion: though the Siddha teaching was a 'closed' and esoteric doctrine, it was not socially 'closed' and exclusive; in direct opposition to the Hindu orthodoxy, no distinction at all is made here with regard to the caste or even nationality of the 'preceptors'.

12. *Cittar Ñāṉakkōvai*, ed. by M. V. Venugopala Pillai, Madras, Premier Art Press.

13. *Cittar periya ñāṉakkōvai eṉa vaḷaṅkum cittar pāṭalkaḷ*, ed. by Aru. Rāmanātaṉ, Madras, Prema Arts Printers.

14. Cf. also Heinrich Nau, *Prolegomena zu Pattanattu Pillaiyars Padal* (Halle, 1919): '. . . die Werke der Sidhars [sind] von śivaistischen Zeloten, besonders den Paṇḍārams, systematisch verfälscht und beseitigt worden.'

15. *Tibetan Printed Scrolls*, Rome, 1949, p. 226.

16. *Indian Historical Quarterly*, IV, 2 (1928) 187–96. The author tried to show that *sandhā* in *sandhāvacaṉa*, *sandhābhāṣā*, as such language is called, stands for *sandhāya* 'aiming at, intending'.

17. In Sanskrit tantric texts, *śaśin* or *candra* 'moon' stands (or can stand) for *śukla* 'sperm', for *iḍā* 'left conduit', for *prajñā* 'perfect wisdom' etc.; while *ravi* (in our Tamil text the loanword *iravi* is actually used) 'sun' (also *sūrya*) may stand for *rajas* (menses, menstrual blood), for *piṅgalā* 'left conduit', for *upāya* 'means'.

18. St. 221.

19. St. 52.

20. *mōṉa nilaiyiṉil mutti uṇṭām* 'truly there is Liberation in the State of Silence' (Iṭaikkāṭṭuc Cittar 98).

21. *cūṉiyam*, e.g. in Iṭaikkāṭṭuc Cittar 2, see below; or *pāḻveḷi* 'empty, devastated plain', *ib.* 81.

22. e.g. Civavākkiyar 9, see below.

23. More about Yoga as an integral part of tantrism and of Siddha techniques will be said in Chapter 11.

NOTES TO CHAPTER 3

24. *Tirumantiram* 1463 (1490).

25. The entire Chapter 7 is dedicated to *siddhis.*

26. Briggs, George W., *Gorakhnāth and the Kānphaṭā Yogīs*, Calcutta, 1938, p. 226.

27. Dasgupta Shashibhusan, *Obscure Religious Cults and Background of Bengali Literature*, Calcutta, 1946, 245 ff.

NOTES TO CHAPTER 4

28. For those who are interested in Indian medicine one can recommend J. Filliozat's *La doctrine classique de la médecine indienne*, Paris, 1949, and *Magie et médecine*, Paris, 1943, by the same author.

29. Cf. st. 1823: *uḷḷam peruṅkōyil ūṉ uṭampu ālayam.*

30. *Yogasūtras* II, 40.

31. The plants are classified into *ceṭi* 'shrubs', *koṭi* 'creepers', *maram* 'trees', *pillu* 'grasses' and *pūṇṭu* 'herbs'. The anorganic substances into *āṇcarakku* 'male substances' and *peṇcarakku* 'female substances', on account of which they are susceptible to combination.

32. Agastya and his works will be discussed in some detail below.

33. Cf. Robert's *Oriental Illustrations of the Sacred Scriptures*, p. 281, *English Encyclopaedia, Biography*, Vol. III, p. 87, Taylor, W., *Oriental Historical Manuscripts* I, pp. 135, 172, 175, *Madras Journal of Literature and Science*, Vol. IX, p. 161 (Brown).

34. See below.

35. All these postures have been described and explained by modern Western exponents of Haṭha Yoga, some of them solid and serious enough, like R. Hittleman or M. Volin.

36. *pirāṇaṉ pōyviṭṭa nilai maraṇam.*

37. According to Western medicine, it is 18/min.

38. It is a fact that animals that breathe more rapidly than man tend to be more restless and short-lived (e.g. monkeys), whereas slow-breathing animals (e.g. elephants, tortoises) are long-lived.

39. He always reminded his patients that in moments of stress, emotional disturbances, harassments and the like, they should deliberately slow down their rate of breathing, whereby nervousness will decrease, composure will be regained, and this will also have a beneficial effect on the entire neuro-vegetative system. The one breathing exercise which he recommended most often was the 'healing breath' directed to the spine: Lie on the back, completely relaxed, place both hands, palms down, upon the *maṇipūra cakra* (solar plexus, in the region of the navel.) Inhale slowly, and with each calm and deep exhalation send the *prāṇa* (or rather imagine sending it) down the spine and into the solar plexus. It is true that after a while one feels some warmth along the spine and a kind of refreshment as if the tiredness was 'washed away' by a 'shower' of *prāṇa*.

40. The combination of the postures would depend on the nature of the patient's complaint: thus e.g. for hangover (not necessarily post-alcoholic, but also emotional) he would recommend the 'plough' (*kalappai*), the 'shoulder pose (*carvaṅkācaṉam*) and the 'fish' (*mīṉ*), in this order.

41. *Voyages de François Bernier*, II, 130, Engl. version cited according to M. Eliade, *op. cit.* p. 275.

NOTES TO CHAPTER 5

42. Cf. *Śatapatha Brāhmaṇa* III, 8, 27 and elsewhere: *amṛtam āyur hiraṇyam.*

43. *op. cit.* p. 281.

44. The division of 'substances' (*carakku*) into *āṇcarakku* 'male substances' and *peṇcarakku* 'female substances' which sometimes occurs in the symbolism and imagery even in the Siddha poems, is interesting and suggests the Chinese binomial *yin-yang* speculation. It is possible that the Chinese Taoist alchemists imitated the Indian Buddhist tantric masters, but it is also possible that Tamil alchemy underwent Chinese influence (cf. J. Filliozat, *JA*, CCXXIII, 1963, 110–12 and *Dan Viet-nam*, III, Aug. 1949, 113–10). Cf. M. Eliade, *op. cit.* p. 416. My Siddha informant maintained that in this division is revealed a modern-like knowledge of chemistry, *āṇcarakku* being equivalent to 'alkaline-based ingredients' and *peṇcarakku* being equivalent to 'acids'. For Indian alchemy cf. Rāy, Prafulla Chandra, *A History of Hindu Chemistry*, 2nd ed., Calcutta, 1904–1909, and Mookerjee, R. K., *Rasa-jala-nidhi; or, Ocean of Indian Chemistry and Alchemy*, Calcutta, 1926–38.

NOTES TO CHAPTER 6

45. 'The Self is Pure Consciousness . . . There is only one Consciousness and this, when it identifies itself with the body, projects itself through the eyes and sees the surrounding obects . . . The Self is the pure Reality . . . When all thoughts are stilled, pure Consciousness remains' (Ramaṇa Mahārṣi).

46. 'The spiritual heart-centre is quite different from the blood-propelling muscular organ known by the same name. The spiritual heart-centre is not an organ of the body' (Ramaṇa Mahārṣi).

47. For details concerning these psychosomatic problems, the interested reader should consult the following publications (apart from the book of Dr. Brosse:): Laubry, Ch. and Brosse, T., 'Documents recueillis aux Indes sur les "yogins" par l'enregistrement simultané du pouls, de la respiration et de l'électrocardiogramme', *Presse médicale*, Paris, LXXXIII, 14 October 1936; Bagchi, B. K., Wenger, M. A., 'Correlations électrophysiologiques de certains exercices yogiques', *Compte rendu du 1er Congrès international des sciences neurologiques de Bruxelles*, 21–28.6.1957, Vol. 3, Pergamon Press, 1959; Das, M. N., Gastaut, H., 'Variations de l'activité électrique de cerveau, du coeur et des muscles squelettiques au cours de la méditation et de l'extase yogique', *Conditionnement et réactivité en électroencephalographie*, Paris, Masson, 1957, 211–18; Satyanarayanamurti, G. V. M. D., Brahmayya,

P., Sastri, M. B. B. S., 'A preliminary scientific investigation into some of the unusual manifestations acquired as a result of Yogic practices in India', *Wiener Zeitschrift für Nervenheilkunde und deren Grenzgebiete*, Wien, Springer, 1958; Filliozat, Jean, 'Les limites des pouvoirs humains dans l'Inde', in *Limites de l'humain*, Paris, 1943, 23–8; id., 'Sur la "concentration oculaire" dans le Yoga', *Yoga* (Harburg-Wilhelmsburg) I (1931) 93–102; Anand, B. K., China, G.S., 'Investigations on Yogis claiming to stop their heart beats', *Ind. Journal of Medical Research* 49, 1 January 1961, 90–4. There exist interesting parallels between Yoga and the therapeutic method of 'autogene training' ('autodeconcentration by concentration') as evolved by J. H. Schulz, cf. Johannes H. Schulz, *Das autogene Training* (*Konzentrative Selbstentspannung*), 10th ed., Stuttgart, 1960.

48. The traditional ten *nāḍīs* in Tamil Siddha texts: *iṭaikalai, piṅkalai, cuḻūmuṇai, kāntāri, atti, ciṅkuvai, alampuṭai, puruṭan, caṅkini, kuru.*

49. Perhaps the *nāḍīs* and *cakras* 'exist' so to say 'physically' in the sphere of anti-matter, as was pointed out to me by a Western-oriented and sophisticated Siddha yogin.

50. Kuṇḍalinī is 'identified' by some modern-oriented yogis with the parasympatic nervous system, with the pneumogastric automatic activities which, in Yoga, become voluntarily controlled.

51. Anal contraction: the anal sphincters are forcibly contracted, the abdomen pulled in simultaneously, the chin pressed against the chest, and the diaphragm pushed up toward the thorax.

52. Which reminds us of the ancient Greek pneumatist cosmophysiology, and of the speculations about the Holy Spirit of Christianity.

53. Theos Bernard, *Hatha-Yoga, The Report of a Personal Experience*, New York, 1944. The German translation was published in Stuttgart in 1957 under the title *Hatha Yoga, Ein Erfahrungsbericht aus Indien und Tibet.*

54. The rhythm usually recommended being 1:4:2=inspiration:retention:expiration.

55. Cf. T. Brosse, *op. cit.* pp. 123–24: 'Le "mystère" de la respiration, carrefour oú se recontrent les activités physiologiques, psychologiques et spirituelles, fonction qui exprime sur son propre plan l'activité des niveaux sus-jacents et qui possède aussi le pouvoir, sinon de les induire, du moins de les favoriser. La respiration doit recéter pour les sciences humaines de profonds secrets biologiques et le yoga nous offre une occasion unique de déchiffrer ses difficiles leçons' (p. 123). 'Nous sommes convaincue maintenant du rôle primordial de la respiration et de la précision de son langage aussi bien que de celui des ondes à périodicité respiratoire qui traduisent un

même état fonctional neuro-végétatif, en relation avec la fonction psychique' (p. 124).

56. In 'modernised' and up-dated (yet perfectly sound and genuine) instructions for meditative practice, like those given by Śrī Ramaṇa Mahāṛṣi, *japa* or uttering the names of gods, and *mantras* like *oṃ*, verbally or mentally, 'with feeling of devotion', is considered as a technique to 'keep out all other thoughts except the one thought of OM or God. All incantations and invocations help to do that. . . . Invocation really means clinging to one thought to the exclusion of all others. That is the purpose of it. It leads to absorption which ends in Self-realization.' However, Śrī Ramaṇa says: 'There is no difference between God and His name.' Here we have indeed a recent confirmation of the basic tantric tenet: a *mantra is* the object which it represents.

57. L. Renou—J. Filliozat, *L'Inde classique*, 568.

NOTES TO CHAPTER 7

58. Vācaspatimiśra's Comm. on *Yogasūtra* III. 24.

59. It is interesting to note here Śrī Ramaṇa Mahāṛṣi's attitude to the *siddhis*. Question: 'On realizing *samādhi*, does not one obtain *siddhis* also?' Answer: 'In order to display *siddhis*, there must be others to recognize them. That means, there is no *jñāna* (knowledge) in the one who displays them. Therefore, *siddhis* are not worth a thought: *jñāna* alone is to be aimed at and gained' (*Maharshi's Gospel*, 8th ed., 1969, p. 32). And elsewhere: 'Enlightened enquiry alone leads to Liberation. Supernatural powers are all illusory appearances created by the power of *māyā*. Self-realization which is permanent is the only true accomplishment (*siddhi*)' (*Collected Works*, 3rd ed., 1968, p. 75). And again: 'People who desire powers (*siddhis*) are not content with their idea of Pure Consciousness. They are inclined to neglect the supreme happiness of Realization for the sake of powers. In search of these they follow by-lanes instead of the high road and so risk losing their way' (*The Teachings*, 2nd ed., 1965, p. 233). My own Siddha informant was most reluctant to demonstrate his *siddhis*; but he did in the end, displaying in a most effective way the *siddhi* of *vaśitva*.

NOTES TO CHAPTER 8

60. *vaicca veccil tē<u>n</u>alō vaṇṭi <u>n</u>eccil pūvalō/ kaiccu tāvil vaittuṭa<u>n</u> karaṇṭa pālu meccilē.*

61. Civavākkiyar, st. 27.

62. Iṭaikkāṭṭuc Cittar, 22.

63. Kutampaic Cittar.

64. St. 26.

65. St. 11.

NOTES TO CHAPTER 9

66. *Nalvaḷi*, 2.

67. A. V. Subramania Aiyar, *op. cit.* p. 82.

NOTES TO CHAPTER 10

68. Notes by T. P. Meenakshisundaram to Simon Casie Chitty's *The Tamil Plutarch*, ed. 1946.

69. Cf. Notes by T. P. Meenakshisundaram (ed. *The Tamil Plutarch*, 1946): 'Agastya as a historical figure is no more than a will o' the wisp but as a tradition he wields an influence which is felt in all walks of Tamilian life.'

70. That *this* Siddha Agastya was a very late author may be seen from his medical works in which he speaks of syphillis as *paraṅkiviyāti*, 'the Frankish disease'.

71. *yōkac camātiyi<u>n</u> uḷḷē yakaliṭam/ yōkac camātiyi<u>n</u> uḷḷē yuḷaroḷi/ yōkac camāti-yi<u>n</u> uḷḷē yuḷacatti/ yōkac camāti yukantavar cittarē.*

72. Interestingly enough, the term Siddhānta (*cittāntam*) is used for the first time in this text, e.g. in st. 963.

73. *aṉpum civamum iraṇṭeṉpar arivilār/ aṉpē civamāva tārum arikilār/ aṉpē civamāva tārum arintapiṉ/ aṉpē civamāy amarntirun tārē.*

74. *uṭampār aḻiyil uyirār aḻivar/ tiṭampaṭa meyññāṉam cēravu māṭṭār/ uṭampai vaḷarkkum upāyam arintē/ uṭampai vaḷartteṉ uyirvaḷar ttēṉē.*

75. *uḷḷam peruṅkōyil ūṉ uṭampu ālayam.*

76. 705.

77. *lotus*= the most typical posture used for meditation; *svastikāsana*= a sitting cross-legged posture, preparation for the lotus.

78. One of the four chief postures (*siddha*, *padma*, *siṃha* and *bhadra*) mentioned already in the *Yogatattva Upaniṣad*. A meditation-posture.

79. The body in the Lotus posture is raised and rests on palms, supported by arms, thrust down through the crossed legs.

80. The Lion or *siṃha*: an imitation of a roaring lion, cf. e.g. R. Hittleman, *Yoga*, 1964, p. 218.

81. Cf. e.g. J. Stearn, *Yoga, Youth and Reincarnation*, 1968, p. 309.

82. Another simple and easy sitting pose, cf. e.g. R. Hittleman, *op. cit.* p. 78, Fig. 81.

83. A simple and comfortable cross-legged position, cf. e.g. J. Stearn, *op. cit.* p. 312.

84. *namaṉukku iṭamillai* (787) 'there is no place for Naṉam (= Sanskrit Yama 'Death').

85. *pariyaṅkayōkam* (e.g. 810).

86. The hour is a *kaṭikai* of 24 minutes, not 'our' hour of 60 minutes.

87. Usually, *semen virile* is termed *veḷḷi* (e.g. 806), i.e. 'silver; the white substance; Friday, while *semen muliebre* is termed *viyāḻam* 'Thursday'.

88. 810.

89. 813.

90. Tamil *kaḷḷattaṭṭāṉ*.

91. *kuḷal*, i.e. penis.

92. Tamil *amuri*.

93. According to a personal communication from one of my *siddhāchāryas*, what is meant here is the masculine sperm which, when swallowed, mixed with pepper, is of great rejuvenating power. A mixture of man's sperm and the discharge of the woman should also be licked and swallowed, for the same or even greater therapeutic and rejuvenating effects. Though cunni-

lingus and fellatio (oral sex) are usually discouraged or even abhorred by classical Indian erotic texts, in later literature, and in Tantric Siddha practice (at least in the South) they have quite an important place.

94. Apart from borrowing the Sanskrit terms *bindu* and *'śukla.*

95. Apart from borrowing the Sanskrit terms *nāda* or *soṇita.*

96. Male generative organ.

97. Of what has been termed 'henolocotheism'.

98. However, he is against sects and their feuds (1545, 1568).

99. *nāṉ peṟṟa iṉpam peṟuka ivvaiyakam* 'Let this world obtain the bliss which I obtained.'

100. A. V. Subramania Aiyar, *op. cit.* p. 34.

101. Such as *aṇṭam* 'sky', *akaṇṭam* 'all, entireness', *cōti* 'light', *catā* 'always', *campiratāyam* 'tradition', *cāttiram* 'science' etc.

102. as *cittamār civavākkiya tēvar.*

103. T. P. Meenakshisundaram, *A History of Tamil Literature*, 1965, 70.

104. i.e. *ci, va, ya, na, ma* which, taken together, produce the very sacred mantra *śivāyanama* 'Obeisance to Śiva'.

105. The Three Primeval Ones are Brahma the Creator, Viṣṇu the Preserver, and Śiva the Destructor, who form the Hindu Trinity (*Trimūrti*).

106. i.e. Viṣṇu.

107. These colours, packed with different connotations, stand for the phenomenal world of shapes and colours. Among other connotations, white is associated with the male creativeness (the colour of the sperm; *cukkilam* means both 'whiteness' and 'sperm') as well as the Śivite sacred ash; red with the female principle (the colour of menstrual blood); black, e.g. with the venom which Śiva drank; or, with the darkness of the womb.

108. *citti, siddhi* is the term used in the text.

109. Again, *śivāyanama*, the powerful *mantra.* The five elements which form the material of this world including the physical body, are fire, air, earth, water, and ether. Death is considered as the dissolution of the five elements (*pañcatam*).

110. i.e. Śiva as the Cosmic Dancer, performing his dance in the Hall of the temple of Chidambaram. Śiva as the Cosmic Dancer seems to be a purely Tamil concept; images of Lord Nataraja are found only in Tamilnad temples, or in temples built elsewhere under Tamil influence.

111. Lingam (rubbed with vermilion), the phallus, is one of the images used in Hindu temples to represent (the creative power of) Śiva.

112. One of the most emphatic denials of the ageless, classical Hindu doctrine of reincarnation, valid almost universally in all Indian systems of religious philosophy.

113. Cf. Chapter 6.8.

114. Tamil *tirunīṟu, nīṟu* 'sacred ashes made by burning cow-dung'; one of the symbols of Śiva and śaivism. Devoted Śaivites use it on their forehead, sometimes also on their chests and arms.

115. Circumambulating the stone-image of gods and adorning them with flowers are basic components of orthodox Hindu ritual, both at home and in temples.

116. Hinduism, too, has its demons and devils, who sometimes accompany the dreadful goddess Kālī and/or the god of death Yama, and feed on corpses.

117. C. and H. Jesudasan, *A History of Tamil Literature*, p. 227.

118. *ib.*, p. 227.

119. By 'sleepless sleep' is meant the stilling of the mind. Cf. in this connection the following lines from *Day by day with Bhagavan*, by A. Devaraja Mudaliar (1968), p. 178: 'By "sleep" should be understood, he told me, "the sleepless sleep" we often hear mentioned in Tamil books, e.g. *tūṅkāmal tūṅkic cukam peṟuva tekkālam* When will I attain the bliss of sleeping, yet not sleeping?' In fact, as we may see, the Maharshi quotes here couplet 2 of Pattirakiriyar. This indicates the Maharshi's intimate knowledge of Siddha writings.

120. *Kōyil nāṉmaṇimālai, Tirukkaḻumala mummaṇikkōvai, Tiruviṭaimarutūr mummaṇikkōvai, Tiru Ēkāmpamuṭaiyār tiruvantāti, Tiruvoṟṟiyūr orupā orupaḵtu.*

121. A full translation of Paṭṭiṉattār's poetry will hopefully be prepared by the present author in the near future.

122. The nine 'entrances' to human body: 2 eyes, 2 ears, 2 nostrils, mouth, anus and genitals.

123. The eternal cosmic order and the moral order of things.

124. Brahma: the highest deity of the Hindu Trinity, the Creator. Has four faces. In Sanskrit Brahmā. Must be distinguished from Sanskrit Brahma (neuter) which means 'the absolute', and from Brahman (Sanskrit Brahmā), the member of the priestly caste.

125. There are some formulae which recur again and again in the writings of the Tamil Siddhas. There is e.g. this constantly repeated metaphor, repeated almost *verbatim*, to give expression to the idea of the impermanence of this life which is compared to the 'bubble (on the surface) of water'. We find it in Pattirakiri 62, in Paṭṭiṉattār *Mutalvaṉ Muṟaiyīṭu* 14 ('the body

which is just a bubble of water'), in Kaṭuveḷic Cittar 3 ('this body is but bubble on the surface of water') etc. etc.

126. That is bitter, sweet, sour, salty, astringent (*tuvar*) and hot (as spices, *kār*).

127. This lengthy poem has been ascribed previously to the famous medieval poet Aruṇakiri.

128. past, present and future.

129. The desire of earth (*maṇ*), gold (*poṉ*) and women (*peṇ*).

130. The gross physical body, the fine body underlying the physical body, and the 'anti-body', the body in the world of anti-matter.

131. The original says *carkuru* (Skt. *sadguru*), i.e. the true spiritual preceptor.

132. *Kutampai* is an earthen ring worn by Tamil women to widen the perforation in their ear-laps.

133. In Spoken Tamil, *veṭṭaveḷiccam* means 'broad daylight' but also 'something evident'. Cf. also the following Tamil proverb: 'If one keeps the fist closed, what may be inside is a secret, but if one opens the hand, all is clear' (*veṭṭaveḷi*).

134. This form is called *kaṇṇi*, lit. 'flower-bud'.

135. i.e. the Tamil of prose, of lyrical poetry, and of dramatic poetry.

136. i.e. a combination of dried ginger, dried pepper and *Piper longum* (*pippili, tippili*).

137. A combination of cardamom, pepper, *Piper longum*, dried ginger, *Eugenia caryophyllaea*, and *takkōlam* which is probably *Piper cubeba*, but can also mean the flower of *Calyptranthes jambolana*.

138. The three works in question are the *Tirikaṭukam*, the *Cirupañcamūlam*, and the *Ēlāti*. They belong to the late Old Tamil literary period.

139. Cf. a Tamil saying 'To peel twenty-four skins off a fresh onion' used of something complicated or difficult, but also about a hypercritical person.

140. Cf. the Tamil proverb 'However many perfumes you put on an onion it will still emit a bad smell.'

141. This stanza, and the four following it, have been so popular that they became a true folk-song.

142. It would indeed deserve a special, very minute examination, which cannot naturally be attempted here.

143. To give just a single instance: the word *oyil* 'graceful movement' (in st. 50, 56) is first used by the great medieval poet Aruṇakiri (1400–1450 A.D.).

144. Which may, however, be an earlier work, of the 14th Century.

145. The mountains which exist in the India conceived as a partly mythical, legendary country.

146. The seven legendary, half-mythical oceans.

147. heaven, earth and the infernal regions.

148. A fabulous mountain said to be situated in the centre of the earth.

149. This stanza expounds a series of Yogic techniques: one must penetrate into the Heart of the 'subtle' body, start a 'fire' by breathing in and out, so that the vital energy, *prāṇa*, is activated in the 'net' of the *nāḍīs* or 'conduits', get rid of false, illusory perceptions, and perform concentration by 'gazing' at the *ājñācakra*, the seat of mind and intelligence.

150. It was said above that the Siddha yogin does the opposite of what life demands of him. This concerns social attitudes as well, and stanza 123 is expressive of this rejection of the 'decent' ways of established society.

NOTES TO CHAPTER 11

151. *Day by Day with Bhagavan*, ed. 1968, p. 116.

152. *ib.* p. 162.

153. Also known as *Kōrakkar mūvikai*. This Indian counterpart of marihuana is more frequently known as *kañcā*.

154. I would like to mention as a kind of promise for the future the serious interest a few doctors and psychiatrists in Holland have shown recently in Siddha doctrines and practices.

155. A great number of stanzas ascribed to Tēraiyar may also be found in a large encyclopaedia of medical subjects entitled *Patārttakuṇa cintāmaṇi* (1504 stanzas).

156. *karaṇai*, a plant of different species; I was unable to identify it. *Dracontium*?

157. A medicine prepared from the juice of certain herbs and taken by the nose to promote the discharge of mucus.

158. Black paint for the eyes.

159. *Proceedings of the Second International Conference-Seminar of Tamil Studies*, Madras, I, 1971, 169.

160. Thames and Hudson, London, 1963.